Surprise!
Now You're A
Software
Project Manager

Surprise!
Now You're A
Software
Project Manager

Bas De Baar

First Edition

Multi-Media
Publications Inc.
Lakefield, Ontario

Surprise! Now You're a Software Project Manager
by Bas De Baar

Acquisitions Editor: Kevin Aguanno
Copy Editing: Josette Coppola
Typesetting: Tak Keung Sin
Cover Design: Cheung Hoi

Published by:
Multi-Media Publications Inc.
R.R. #4B, Lakefield, Ontario, Canada, K0L 2H0

http://www.mmpubs.com/

ISBN (Paperback):   1-895186-75-7
ISBN (Adobe PDF ebook):   1-895186-76-5
ISBN (Microsoft LIT ebook):   1-897326-77-3
ISBN (Palm PDB ebook):   1-897326-79-X
ISBN (Mobipocket PRC ebook):   1-897326-78-1

Published in Canada.

Library and Archives Canada Cataloguing in Publication

De Baar, Bas
          Surprise! Now you're a software project manager / Bas De Baar.
-- 1st ed.

Includes bibliographical references.
Also available in electronic format.
ISBN 1-895186-75-7

          1. Computer software--Development--Management.
2. Project management. I. Title.

QA76.76.D47D42 2006   005.1068'4   C2006-902757-9

Table of Contents

Dedication

This One Goes Out to the One I Love

Acknowledgements

In August of 2005, I came in contact with Kevin Aguanno of Multi-Media Publishing. He asked me if I was interested in updating my previous book, *The Microwave Way to Software Project Management,* and publishing it with his Canadian company. Saying yes was the easy part. I had written a lot of short pieces after the original version was printed, so I had no problem in deciding what new material to add to my work. What was meant as just a short update resulted in a complete restructuring and rewriting, mutilation beyond recognition. I would like to thank Kevin for inviting me to write this book and giving me his full support. Without these two considerations, this book would never have been written.

Being Dutch has its disadvantages. I'm not a native English speaker, as you might have guessed. A lot of people have contributed their efforts to make the original text understandable in the English language. I would especially like to thank Josette Coppola from Multi-Media Publishing, who had the tedious task of making a readable book out of these ramblings of mine that I call a manuscript.

Finally, I would like to thank my wife, Simone, who supports me every day and puts up with me when my mind wanders off, thinking about how or what to write. I'm always grateful that she doesn't mind watching movies on DVD while I am spending time behind my laptop.

Preface

Have you ever woken up thinking, *How did I get here?* I'm not referring to uncertainty about where you are physically but to concern over the status of your project activities. One morning, you had a delay in your software project on your hands. Thinking back, you know how the assignment fell behind schedule, as all assignments do, one day at a time. And the worst part is that you know how it could have been avoided, or at least kept from escalating into the situation you now face on this particular morning. You know what you could have done to prevent the delay, and yet you didn't do it.

If you have woken up like this on one or more mornings, we share some similar experiences. I know what to do. I know the best procedures by heart. But sometimes it seems that the heart is a long way from the brain. Attempts are made, more then once, but there is always that morning.

This book started out as my personal vendetta against all mornings of waking up preoccupied with worries about a project. It first appeared a couple of years ago as a small book called *The Microwave Way to Software Project Management*. While writing the content of that original book, I kept one thing in mind: *if you had only one day to talk about software project management, what would you say?* I surely wouldn't be yapping about great graphs.

Some years have now gone by. I spent more time in the project trenches implementing information systems, and I got hooked on some new, emerging techniques that I thought might help me out. My interest was actually fired up by the debate between modernists who favored new agile approaches and traditionalists who supported the plan-driven method of tackling projects. I thought that both sides were right.

How can that be? Did I miss something? Is someone from one or the other group lying?

The reason for my confusion at that time lay in a footnote to the stories of the two camps: both approaches work well, under the right circumstances. But what makes up those circumstances?

As I'm a technically oriented person by education, my first reaction was to consider the difficulties of the system being constructed. Of course that is one important aspect to a project's success, but after taking in a deep breath and a nice cup of coffee, it all came back to me. What really makes all the difference in a project? People.

Managing software projects in organizations is a people-intensive process. The fears and wishes of stakeholders determine the path that the project will follow. If you look at the subject from that point of view, the obvious becomes even clearer: every method or technique ever invented is an attempt to address a certain problem or reduce the risk that a specific event will take place. Progress reports provide managers with feedback on issues such as how the project is going, whether too much money is being spent, and how many delays are at hand. Putting a developer and a user close to each other is a way to prevent communication problems that can occur when a cold paper trail is used. And so on and so forth.

If different techniques solve different problems and each project is unique, can there be one correct way of managing a software project? Of course not, and that is exactly why I agreed with both agile and plan-driven supporters in our industry.

So I picked up the old word processor again and set out an updated goal for the book that now lies before you: *if you had only one weekend to talk about software project management, what would you say?* (You see, I added a full day in respect to the previous book.) I would tell you about stakeholders and how they operate in a project, I would tell you about risks, and I would tell you about the basic problems you try to solve as a software project manager.

In this book I explain how stakeholder analysis and risk management provide you with the means to analyze the project circumstances. After that, I show you how you can tailor a project approach that should at least cover the basic risks you must address to manage a successful project. You see, even if I have an entire weekend with you, I will try to avoid yapping about graphs. With Internet resources nowadays, you can find techniques and methods all over the place. The difficulty lies in knowing what you have to look for, and to know that you must have a clue about what problems you are trying to solve.

The content of this book was written by me as an individual, based upon my own ideas and experiences, and it therefore represents my own opinions. There is no connection whatsoever between this book and any company or organization.

Book Overview

In this section I provide a summary of the chapters in this book.

Chapter 1: Introduction

I once saw a program on public television that revealed how magic tricks are performed and explained how magicians saw a woman in half. Ever since then, David Copperfield bores me. Learning how acts of illusion are accomplished will shatter your dreams. As software projects take place in reality, dreaming is not an option, and therefore it's very profitable to understand the workings behind the tricks of the stakeholders concerned in the project (if you find this a weird twist in a sentence, wait until you read the rest).

Stakeholders are all the people involved in a project: the customer, the supplier, the boss, the user, you name it. As a project manager, you have to deal with all of them, and, even worse, these people will determine if your software project will be a success or a failure. This first chapter describes an image that should be engraved in every software project manager's mind. If you see it, you will surely recognize it. It's short and simple, so much easier to keep in your head than the picture of a huge binder crammed with pages about various methods.

Chapter 2: Project Potion

In spite of what you might think, there is no one magical way to carry out software project management. There is no universal approach that works every time and on every occasion. Every project consists of different people and distinct circumstances. You should design the ideal approach for a certain project based upon all the methods and techniques that are available. You should mix and match, cut and paste from every approach that sounds reasonable, creating your own magical Project Potion in this way.

In this chapter I outline the basic process for designing a specific project approach, using stakeholder analysis and risk management as input and applying project strategy, project organization, and feedback mechanisms as the means to create the most suitable method.

Chapter 3: Stakeholder Analysis

From the start of this book to the very end, I keep on emphasizing the importance of stakeholders in and around a project, but to do something proactive with this understanding, you need to analyze the stakeholders. Yes, you have to put on your psychologist hat and play the shrink.

There are ways to identify all the stakeholders involved and gain some insights into what they want from the project and how they are most likely to operate. You can use this knowledge to your advantage, as it will shape both your project organization and the way you communicate with each and every one of the stakeholders.

Chapter 4: Risk Management

I cannot tell you what the future will bring. No one can predict what will happen with any certainty, although some people believe they have the power to do so. This whole project concept is based on assumptions and estimations, on guesses and hunches. Sometimes we are wrong, and while working on a project we have to deal with this as a fact of life. Enter *risk management*. A risk is the possibility of loss of some kind, and it's all about the potential for conditions to be different from what you believe them to be right now. Risk involves not only whatever can go wrong but also whatever may arise if the future brings something unexpected. "Dealing with Uncertainty" would be a good subtitle for this chapter.

Chapter 5: Tailoring the Approach

Using risk management and stakeholder analysis, you will collect a lot of information about the stakeholders and the uncertainties in general surrounding your project. This chapter goes back to the basic ingredients for a proper project approach and explains how you can put them together to handle the data collected in the previous chapters.

I then tell you how:

- Business priorities and uncertainties (risks) can be resolved by using the proper strategy and feedback with the stakeholders

- Insight into stakeholder interests can result in the optimum project organization and correct feedback mechanisms about the process and the product

Chapter 6: Getting the Requirements for the Product

Whatever you do or whatever you make, know all you can about doing it or making it. After an initial analysis, the global contours of the project are outlined by goals and scope. You should get more specific, though, and being explicit about the requirements related to the product is what this chapter is all about.

Chapter 7: Getting the Requirements for the Process

We could name this the "party-pooper" section: it is about the constraints that stakeholders put on the process, such as budgetary restrictions or time limits.

Chapter 8: Feedback on the Product

As a kid, I played this little game at school called *Telephone Line*. Twenty children huddled into a circle and one of us started by whispering a sentence into the ear of the neighboring kid, so that no one else could hear what was said. The message would be whispered from one child to the next in succession until it had come "'round circle." The fun of the game was in comparing what the last kid heard to what the first one originally said. Usually, the two sentences didn't even come close to sounding the same.

While the project is underway, the requirements stated in the beginning should be validated. This process addresses two points: are the initial requirements still valid, and are we meeting them? This chapter discusses the requirements set for the product part of the project.

Chapter 9: Feedback on the Process

In Holland, we have this huge (200 kilometer) ice-skating event, the Elf Steden Tocht, which in English means "Eleven Cities Tour." On the course there are a number of checkpoints that are in fact the eleven cities, and you have to get a stamp in each one. Getting these stamps is very important, as the race is actually about passing all the checkpoints.

In a project, it's all about getting the approvals to keep on going. This chapter talks about providing feedback on the requirements set for the process part of the project. Are we still within time and budget limits, and are the project constraints still the same?

Audience

This is a book on software project management, so it is obviously intended for people who either manage software projects or have the ambition to do so in the near future. However, the less formal you are, the more suited this book is for you. I treat the subject in a direct manner, and I try to make the experience as entertaining as possible.

Experienced managers can use this book as a guide to a stakeholder-centered approach to software project management. Students, or project-managers-to-be, can use it as a crash course. It is written by someone who studied the concepts of project management methods, went to work as a project manager, and was totally confused by the differences between the methods and the realities. This book provides the glue that connects what you see in the real world with the techniques that are available to software engineering and project management professionals.

CHAPTER ONE

Introduction

A software project is a very curious thing. Consider what happens when a typical project is launched:

> A man sits at his desk on a Friday afternoon thinking, I want a new accounting system. He calls his contact at the IT department and informs him of his wishes. Just before he hangs up the phone, he adds, "Oh, and by the way, this means that you are the project manager for this assignment. It would be great if you could start on Monday. Have a nice weekend."

> The IT guy—let's call him Hank—stares at the phone he still holds in his hand. He is confused. What new accounting system? What project manager? What Monday? After his first six-pack later that evening, Hank is feeling more relaxed. He can do this. Get a system.

Install it. Nothing to it. He'll make some phone calls first thing on Monday morning and he'll have this project taken care of in no time. As he pops open another brewskie, Hank is feeling empowered.

By Monday, Hank has had the whole weekend to think things over and has decided to contact the accounting department first to get a better idea of what they want. Will just any accounting system serve the purpose, or do they need a specific kind? Who knows?

That Monday morning doesn't go exactly as Hank had planned. He ends up sitting in a room for four hours listening to five employees of the accounting department. He has no clue as to what they are talking about. All he gets from this meeting are the names of five other departments that also use the current accounting system, the names of seven external companies that exchange information with this system, and three huge binders containing memos, short documents, Xeroxes, and handwritten letters explaining "exactly" what the accounting department needs.

Hank spends the remainder of Monday making brief contact with the five other departments and seven other companies whose names he has gotten from the accounting department. After this short round of communications, he can add another twenty names to the list of those who have something to do with the new accounting system.

Reflecting back on these developments later that evening, Hank considers taking a different approach the next day. He'll look into the current system and see what it does. He'll talk a little with his buddies in the IT department to see if they can help him get on the right track.

Tuesday makes Hank's state of mind even worse. From the IT department he gets two additional binders with policies describing which technology and architecture the new system should use, which documentation should be included for the support people, and lots more. Oh, and he can add to his list another ten names of people who have something to say about the new system.

It started out so simple: one man, one statement. After only two days, Hank has a list of over forty people he has to involve and five binders stuffed with what looks like requirements.

I'd like to add that this story is inspired by true events. I have to admit that this case is a little extreme; however, suppose you got such a call on a Friday afternoon. You would have just one weekend for preparation. What should you know for your job as a software project manager? How to make a Gantt chart? How to create large sheets?

It is my opinion that you would be helped most by getting a rundown on the basics, the essence of a software project. If you know the dynamics of a project and how people operate and why, you have almost 80% already covered. You can keep up with the technical stuff as you go along. If you know the "why" of a problem, the "how to solve it" gets a lot easier.

The essential problem of running a project is that you have multiple persons to satisfy, all of them having their own interests in the project, which are not always in perfect harmony with yours. The project manager is faced with the challenge of keeping everyone happy, but often his resources are scarce. Money, time, and people are limited, and in the end a software project is a game of setting priorities and negotiating trade-offs.

Did you notice that I didn't mention even one type of chart in the previous paragraph?

To start you off in the right direction, I talk first in this chapter about the essential mindset of a software project manager. Every project is different, but your primary mindset should remain the same.

In the remainder of this chapter, I address the following two subjects to prepare you for making judgments later on about available methods and techniques (for example, those on the Internet):

- General aspects of methods and some notions about project management and software development processes

- The big question: is there a universal method for all projects? (uh . . . *no*)

Mindset of the Software Project Manager

The thrill of having tickets for the opening night of Andrew Lloyd Webber's new play on Broadway is hard to compare with attending a performance on Amateur Night in our local town hall. Both are plays and both have actors who recite a series of lines to an audience. But ticket prices differ, and the differences in the quality of the players' performances and the stage props may represent quite a gap in relative value. However, is there a difference in terms of the audience's appreciation? Is the evening of those who went to Broadway more memorable than the night of those who didn't cross our county line?

Most people would probably argue that it depends on the expectations of the audience. If theatergoers pay a bundle of money just to see some famous actor, then they should visit Broadway. If all they want to see is a group of folks having some fun as actors, then Amateur Night is surely the way to go. The staging should fit the expectations of the audience, and so all is well.

A project has some aspects common to plays (and not just tragedies). Some tricks are performed by members of a project team (the players) and are closely observed by people with stakes in the project, the stakeholders (the audience). As long as the players perform as expected by the audience, everybody is happy. The principles presented in this section aim at achieving precisely that balance of anticipation and satisfaction. This book covers the subject of *software* projects, and any project that has a larger, software-related element to it can be categorized as such.

One of the central principles introduced in this book is the *flow of the stakes*, which should be the mindset of every project manager. You should "know the flow" and have it mentally imprinted on your brain throughout the project. This is the best way to learn the expectations of all the stakeholders, integrate these different expectations, and ensure that all these people know that their expectations are being met. The main function of this section is to make you aware of this principle of flow that runs throughout every project, but it is not my intention to provide an in-depth analysis of every aspect. Although I try to dig that deeply in later sections, the true depth of flow can only be viewed in practice. Benjamin Hoff reminds us that this is true of many things in life:

> A basic principle of Lao-tse's teaching was that this Way of the Universe could not be adequately described in words, and that it would be insulting both to its unlimited powers and to the intelligent human mind to attempt to do so.[1]

This is perhaps a bit much, but it gives you a certain idea. Think of the flow as the apotheosis of this section, but first we must build up some context.

The Software Project Manager's Problem

The management of a software project is really an art; it's a trick that's difficult to master. The difficulty lies in the central problem the software manager is faced with, appropriately named "the software project manager's problem,"[2] as explained by Barry W. Boehm and Rony Ross. They believe that everyone affected by the project, directly or indirectly, has something to say, again directly or indirectly, and will do so. All of them want to get the best from this project for themselves personally or for their (part of the) organization. It's the job of the software project manager to see that everyone gets what he or she wants, in one way or another. He has to 'make everyone a winner."

In this respect, the role of the project manager becomes that of a negotiator. The customer always wants to have it all for free, the user wants to have the greatest functionality, and the programmer doesn't want to document anything but wants to use the coolest compilers. The software project manager has to make them all happy.

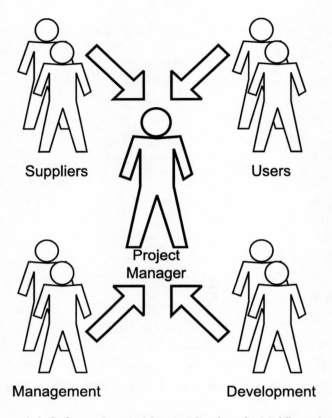

Figure 1-1: Software Project Manager Stuck in the Middle with All the Stakeholders

Focus on the Stakeholders

The entire process of software project management is strongly stakeholder-driven. It's their wishes, fears, dreams—their *stakes*—that determine the course of the project. You have to handle a project to really grasp the impact of people on your endeavor. You have to "live" a project to know the force of political games and power trips. You have to lead a team to cutover under time pressures to appreciate the constructive power of motivated people or the destructive power of demotivated team members. I can keep telling you that people represent the most important aspect of a project, and I can quote statistics or research to convince you that the human factor is the only real concern of a project manager. But you will not really understand this concept unless you have been there yourself.

Once you *have* been there yourself, you'll realize that all the preparation and knowledge in the world will not guarantee success, because there's always that human element, the inescapable fact that people are involved. And in a project, it's the *people* that are the main cause of problems. Time schedules, financial projections, and software goals may be abstractions, but it's the flesh-and-blood people whose work determines your project's status. It's the programmer that misses a deadline and holds up everyone else, it's the financial manager that goes berserk if you can't produce some good budgetary indications, and it's the key user that doesn't give a darn but didn't tell you about his dismal lack of motivation; these are the folks who can cause serious trouble. Issuing the best procedures doesn't mean that people will live by them. You really have to be in the asylum to understand the lunacy of it all. If you haven't been there yet, take this important advice: *focus on the stakeholders.* Be guided by their fears and their wishes.

A *stakeholder* can be a project team member, an employee of the user organization, or a senior manager. It can be virtually anyone, as long as that person has something to do with the project.

I know that this socio/psycho stuff is not the favorite cup of tea among technocrats, but being unknown shouldn't make something scary. In essence, it's even easy to understand. You are part of it. If you are human, you can practice on yourself and try things out on your spouse and kids. Look around your office and try to think about how the situation there is different from the one at home with your kids.

First of all, your children are more transparent than the people at work. They communicate directly what they want, and if they try some power trip on you, you immediately recognize it for what it is. "I want ice cream right now" is pretty clear. If they don't get this very nice cold snack, kids can use crying as a means to get their way. And you may cave in, perhaps just to stop the annoying sound and, of course, the embarrassment of walking through the mall with your yodeling kid.

Let's start to focus on project management.

Your boss or your employees will not be this explicit and predictable. They may try some mind games to manipulate you or (let's avoid being negative) they will have the best intentions, ones you haven't figured out yet.

But in essence, they have the same mechanisms as you and your children. People do what they do to realize their dreams or to avoid having their nightmares come true; in other words, to achieve their wishes or to escape their fears. Within the context of projects, people are the stakeholders.

What people (and stakeholders) really, really, really want are what can be termed their interests or, as I sometimes call them, their stakes (hence the name "stakeholder"; I will use the terms "stakes" and "interests" interchangeably). With fears there is a stake to lose, and with wishes there is something to gain.

In this context, I consider interests as the aspects that drive people. Before you start drawing your "interest evaluation diagram" or some other neat tool or technique, be aware that in general these interests are hardly ever communicated. It's pure mind stuff, all inside the head of the owner. A four-year-old boy may share his true interests with you, but the fifty-year-old graying accountant will tell you nothing.

If no one will tell you anything, what is the point?

People will tell you *something* if you ask them. They will tell you they want an ice cream cone, a new hyperspeed Internet uplink, or a new financial software package. In essence, they tell you what they expect. It is a statement created by *themselves* about a desired situation: their *expectations*.

If I emphasize that expectations are a one-sided communication, then there must be something else as well; enter *requirements*. Requirements are a set of statements negotiated among a group of people. They can be the original expectations, if all agree on the statement itself, but more often than not, requirements consist of some consensus of conflicting expectations.

Requirements are always clearly defined and describe a state that is desired. This is in contrast to expectations, which are generally vague and abstractly formulated.

Interest/Stake	What people really want, not communicated	
Expectation	What people expect or want, communicated	
Requirement	What should be done, negotiated, and communicated	
Interest/Stake	I want that ice cream	Will not lose face again with a delayed project on my hands
Expectation	If I cry and scream, I will get my ice Cream	Will be finished before the start of Q2 next year
Requirement	If you are sweet, you will get ice cream	Total cutover to production finalized before 1/1/20xx

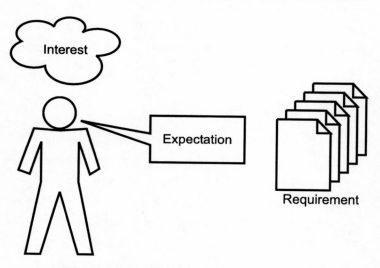

Figure 1-2: People Have Interests and Communicate Expectations that Result in Requirements

Here's an oversimplified example: an interest of a programmer is "to be involved in way cool new technologies like my brother-in-law is" (let's say Java). The corresponding expectation could be, "The system can only be programmed in Java." The expectation can be stated along other technical arguments, but it's only the interest mentioned that caused it to appear. If everyone agrees on this "fact," then "programmed in Java" can become a requirement.

So the project manager has this project, surrounded by requirements that must be met. But remind yourself: they are not the stakes, they are not the crown jewels that may not be touched. So you can mess with the requirements, can't you?

What Is It Worth?

It sounds simple, but getting the expectations is one thing and discovering their corresponding stakes is another. Why bother anyway? What is it worth? A lot. As mentioned earlier, you can't effectively change the stakes, but you can alter the set of requirements as long as the new requirements continue to support the stakes. In this way, there is room to negotiate a set of requirements for the project that poses no conflict, matches the stakes, and thus makes everyone a winner! Right?

Now let's take it one step back. A stakeholder formulates an expectation for the software project; for example, senior management states, "The project should be finished before the end of August." The project manager then has to deal with this time frame. When this deadline is no problem, he can rest assured. However, it's a software project, so the deadline will be a problem. The way to handle it is to get some information on the stakes that prompted this requirement to be formulated in the first place.

Perhaps it's the old "I don't want to lose face when my projects get delayed" concern. That being the case, the project manager can offer alternatives that don't violate the stake, like keeping the deadline but postponing a subsystem. Chances are good that alternative requirements that keep supporting the stakes will be accepted—maybe not easily, but project managers should do something to earn their money.

An example taken from Frederick P. Brooks Jr. illustrates this relationship between stakes and requirements:

> [...] the reluctance to document designs is not due merely to laziness or time pressure. Instead it comes from the designer's reluctance to commit himself to the defense of decisions which he knows to be tentative. By documenting a design, the designer exposes himself to the criticisms of everyone, and must be able to defend everything he writes. If the organizational structure is threatening in any way, nothing is going to be documented until it's completely defensible.[3]

Stakeholders during the Project

The first influence of the stakeholders on the project is usually the most influential, and it occurs at the start of the project. The demands and constraints issued on the process and on the products that are produced set the stage for the entire duration of the software project. The primary task of the project manager should be to reassure the stakeholders that what they communicate is heard and that their stakes are taken care of. Throughout the entire project, the project manager's task consists of giving stakeholders feedback on the state of their requirements.

This feedback can take the following forms:

- Tests
- Test results
- Prototypes
- Reports
- Evaluations
- Plans
- Benchmarks

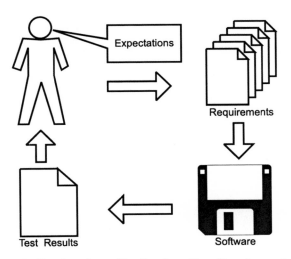

Figure 1-3: Test Results as Feedback on How Requirements Are Translated to Software

This part is essential but easily forgotten. If the project manager does not keep giving feedback, the slightest hint (or rumor) of not sticking to the stakes may set a stakeholder on the warpath against the once so happy project manager.

The Flow of the Stakes

Having said all this, where does it leave the software project manager? In order to have a "happy project," a software project manager should respect the flow of the stakes, as illustrated in the diagram below, and must ensure that stakes go full cycle.

Let's describe this flow in a few steps:

1. Stakeholders have stakes.

2. Stakeholders communicate their stakes by expressing their expectations, which are more formally defined by means of requirements to the process or product.

3. Project management should make every stakeholder a winner by accepting and inventing requirements that continually satisfy the stakes of individual stakeholders and do not conflict with the general process or the product.

4. Project management should give continuous feedback to the stakeholders on the state of the stakes.

5. Based upon this feedback, the expectations and requirements might change, and in this way a new cycle begins.

You Must Know This Flow!

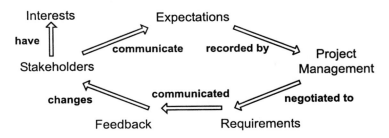

Figure 1-4: The Flow of the Stakes

So now you know the flow. For the coming days, try to fit all that surrounds you into this image of the flow and view the world through these flow-sensitive glasses. As you already might have guessed, the concepts behind the flow are not limited to software projects.

The principles for inventing win-win conditions are discussed in general books like *Getting to Yes* by Roger Fisher and William Ury, who even mention its use in hostage situations.[4] The indirect communication of stakes can even be found in John Gray's *Men Are from Mars, Women Are from Venus.*[5] If a girl tells her boyfriend, "I want you to listen to my problem" (requirement to the process), the stake of the girl typically would be the reduction of her stress by talking about the subject. Unfortunately, the boy's typical interpretation of her stake would be, "She wants me to fix the problem." To understand exactly how this process works, just read the book.

The point I want to make is that you don't have to be currently working on a software project to try The Flow. Try to view as much of life as possible with your glasses colored by the concepts presented. I'm not claiming these concepts should guide your normal life; it is just an exercise! This is still just a book on software project management.

Not Everyone Will Be a Winner

I know this goes against everything I wrote previously, but in reality you will find out that you cannot make all people as happy as they would like to be. You will not be able to satisfy everyone's needs or some people will try to frustrate the project for the simple reason that they just feel like doing so.

However, try to be positive as long as possible. Go the extra mile to make everyone a winner, but be prepared to encounter some negative souls, people who love to play corporate games. You will meet them, but we will cover them in this book, so don't worry.

Don't Forget to Include Yourself!

After you have been "into" the project for a while, you will have read all the paperwork. You will have spoken with a lot of people. You will have asked, "What do you want?" and "What can I do?" When that time comes, it's time for your gut feeling. Do you trust the statements made by the stakeholders? Do you think top management will stick by you? Do you honestly believe the project has a chance to succeed? Now is the time to know. It is late, but you can still get off the train. Once this window of opportunity slams shut, it's your butt that's stuck hanging over the sill. Whenever this project is mentioned, you're the one that people will remember.

It makes no sense to associate yourself with a project if you think it's a *Titanic* or *Mission Impossible IV*. Don't make the mistake of thinking that your efforts will be appreciated even if everything goes down the drain. Failure is an easy thing to remember. The true professionals know their limitations, and the responsible course of action is to either configure the project in such a way that it stands a chance of success or stamp it "return to sender."

A quote is always great, but this one from U.S. Judge Thomas Renfield Jackson's statement to Microsoft's legal counsel during a monopoly trial is in this context almost perfect:

> The code of tribal wisdom says that when you discover you are riding a dead horse, the best strategy is to dismount. In law firms, we often try other strategies with dead horses, including the following: buying a stronger whip; changing riders; saying things like, 'this is the way we have always ridden this horse'; appointing a committee to study the horse; arranging to visit other firms to see how they ride dead horses; increasing the standards to ride dead horses; declaring that the horse is better, faster, and cheaper dead; and finally, harnessing several dead horses together for increased speed.[6]

If you take on a project, don't forget to include your own stakes and be a winner yourself! After all, you are a stakeholder as well!

And if you are a winner and higher management is committed to you as a project manager for the project, make sure they send a memo or an e-mail to all stakeholders, declaring you the head honcho, the big cheese, the ruler of your universe, or something more office-like.

Processes: Project Management versus Software Development

Reality is too difficult for us mortals to comprehend. You think I am kidding you? Try to consider every aspect of the world at the same time. Thinking of the earth may cause you to have a visual image of our planet taken from outer space. Focusing on a particular country may cause your brain to zoom in on one spot. At the same moment you zoom in, you neglect the rest of the earth you just had in your brain. Let's face it: we are not capable of seeing everything.

This is a fact of life, so don't get into a sweat about it. Creative as they are, our brains have found their own ways to deal with it: mostly, by simply neglecting information. As with the example about the earth, our minds can zoom in and zoom out. Another strategy of our brains is to focus on only certain aspects. Think about a nation's geography. Now think about its economics. Most people would get very different visual impressions from these two thoughts. With the first one, I get a mental picture of a topographical map. For the second one, I get images of banks, companies, and the government. We can have different levels of complexity and simplify the levels we use by neglecting certain details.

Why am I bothering you with this? I just want to make you 100% aware that what you are about to read, or ever will read, on the subject of software project management is a representation of a certain level that neglects information about real life situations. Underlying every book on this subject is a specific idea of the real world that explains things to you neatly and cleanly, and (hopefully) in an understandable way. To convey or accept this idea, we simplify and we neglect.

Again, this is no real problem. Heck, we don't even have a choice. Just always be conscious of the assumptions that are made when information is presented in a certain way; always inform yourself about the aspects that are neglected. Project reality will kick you in the back if you don't.

As a software project manager just beginning a job, you want to know what you should do. What should I do, when should I do it, what should other people do, and when? The simplest way to illustrate this phase is by the use of a process description. It will set out a sequence of steps to follow. We in the software industry are suckers for boxes and graphs, so here they are for you:

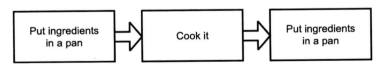

Figure 1-5: A Cooking Process Flow

My process for having a great meal: first, you mix all your ingredients in a pan, next you cook the mixture, and when it is ready you can finally eat it. It's straightforward and simple, with nothing to argue about. Of course, I am assuming you have the ingredients and even a pan. If you want to have a more detailed description, you can include a box before the first one, indicating that you should purchase everything you need before starting to put it in a pan.

There are also no instructions on how to cook it. Of course, it would be very difficult if we just kept on referring to "ingredients" without being more explicit. For more specific directions, we should narrow down what type of meal we are cooking.

I could go on and on about this, but I will not do that to you. Just notice that even a simple process leaves a lot of questions unanswered.

An extra element we introduce in this way of looking at a process is the familiar computer input-output aspect. If a box indicates an activity, it would be nice if this activity resulted in something, the output. And in order to do something, most of the time you need some magic powder to perform it, the input.

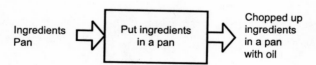

Figure 1-6: Cooking Process with Input and Output

I will let the image speak for itself.

Throughout this book and other texts on the subject, you will note a distinction between the process and the product, between the activities and the items that are produced. A *plan* is a product, like a piece of paper or an MS project file. The process that creates it is called a *planning*.

When focusing on software project management, there are actually two main types of processes involved: the actual creation of the software and the management of the project—the software development process and the project management process, obviously.

If you look at the day-to-day operation of a project, it is sometimes hard to tell that two different processes are involved because they are so closely interconnected. A project management process without a software development process makes no sense (there would be nothing for the project to produce, other than plans and reports), and a software development process without project management would only result in a never-ending, ever-changing process that doesn't fit within the constraints and goals for the project

I make note of this distinction because the failure to appreciate it is sometimes a source of confusion when discussing approaches to software project management. Material written by pure software development people can focus on the software development process and offer only a footnote about the management process, and pure project managers often tell you that a project is a project and so it doesn't matter if you are building a bridge, a spacecraft, or a new accounting system.

In theory, everyone is right; just think about my opening discussion about the brain's way of selectively focusing on or neglecting certain information. In my experience, however, to be an effective software project manager, you have to know and incorporate both the software development process and the project management process.

If you know nothing about software development, it is of course still possible to run the project, but you would have no idea what you were talking about. You would have no clue about what sequence of steps are effective, what the products really are, what problems can occur, and how to tackle them. Software development is still a mystical art. Even though it may seem structured and predictable, sometimes it is not, and ignorance of this fact is what wrecks a project most of the time.

On the other hand, considering project management as merely a footnote may deprive you of great techniques and tips you can pick up from other industries. Although software projects are in their own league, other industries may face similar problems and create effective management solutions for them.

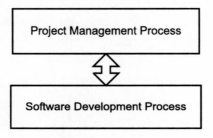

Figure 1-7: Project Management Process versus Software Development Process

In this book I focus on the project management process, but I also beg, borrow, or steal time for software development where needed. And believe me, we will need it a lot, so it is also fair to say that I present an integrated version. Call it whatever sounds more appropriate to you.

One Size Doesn't Fit All

There is no one way to make great lasagna. Of course, the basic idea is always the same, but depending on your tastes, cooking skills, and available ingredients, you can create a lot of variations. Some people use only fresh ingredients, make the pasta from scratch, and spend several hours in the kitchen. I buy prefabricated ingredients and whip up the meal in several minutes. Both dishes are lasagna, but they are very different.

Comparing lasagna to software projects is a stretch, but I'll take my chances. Although some books may lead you to believe that there is only one way to perform a software project, believe me, there isn't. There are many more ways. Just look at the number of methods that are available: Prince2, PMP, Scrum, or Lean Project Management. If you combine these possibilities with the various software development methods that exist, you have plenty of potential combinations that may be useful.

In recent years, there have been some heated debates within the industry about the "right" method of software project management. In one corner you have the traditional *plan-driven* camp, and in the other you find the new rebels, the *agile* supporters. In essence, the first group believes you should define every step that has to be performed in detail up front: the actual task, the timelines, the organization, and the procedures that should be followed. This will increase the predictability, stability, and high assurance of the process and the products it produces. You design a plan, you issue the orders, and you make sure everybody sticks to this original strategy.

The downside of this plan-driven approach is that a software project is never as predictable as everyone hopes, so the cost for this enforced structure is a higher overhead (a lot of time is spent on creating supporting products like plans, reports, and documentation, stuff that is rarely if ever used in the end result). Interest in reducing wasted resources sparked some new ideas about what was the right approach for software projects.

Agile methods differ from plan-driven approaches by assuming that conditions will continually change and addressing this change through the concept of "just enough": just enough structure in the process to keep things going in the right direction and just enough supporting documents like short-range plans and brief reports to meet the current needs. According to this agile philosophy, it makes no sense to attempt to prescribe the future in plans, as the situation will change anyway. Instead, agile managers focus on creating a process that easily adapts to the situation.

Each camp claims that its own approach works better than the other, and both philosophies have great worth. It's hard to argue reasonably against the value of predictability and stability, but adaptiveness also sounds like a very wise strategy. Is a defender of one or another group lying? I will definitely say no. Every method has its merits and every approach can lay claim to a sample project where it worked very effectively. But not every project is the same. Each one involves different people, different tools, different end results, different project constraints, and different circumstances.

Different circumstances require different approaches. If you need creativity to solve a problem or to create a design, you need an easy-going, stimulating approach; if you are racing a deadline to achieve production, a rigid, centralized, and controlled environment is more likely the better way to go. Depending on the environment and general circumstances, a project manager should construct a process and organization that serve him or her best. In the ideal situation, you should be able to cut and paste together a method that suits your particular situation, using approaches that have been proven to work well in the exact situation you find yourself in.

A key question is: what makes up the circumstances of a project?

First of all, the desired end result of the project is a main factor. Creating a navigational system for a spacecraft would be very different from designing an application to organize your recipes. Not only would the application be different in size and complexity, but the requirements on stability and reliability would differ enormously.

Secondly, without hesitation I would say that people represent a major element in the circumstances of a project. In my personal experience, all major problems concerning projects are caused by human factors. It may be just the level of skill or knowledge of a project team member, but don't dismiss too quickly the impact of cultural and political influences on your project.

To give you a better idea, Barry W. Boehm and Richard Turner have defined five dimensions that should affect a method selection:

Criticality: If the end results fail, what would be the cost? The scale ranges from a simple loss of comfort to the loss of many lives.

Personnel: The level of skill of the project team members

Size: The number of personnel involved

Dynamism: The number of requirement changes per month (What is the level of people's ability to define the requirements?)

Culture: Are people accustomed to handling change and taking their own initiative, or are people used to orderliness and having their work laid out in plans for them?[7]

I list these dimensions not to imply that they are the only ones but to illustrate what kind of aspects can influence your choice of a certain approach. And you have to choose. Just as the right approach may be more effective, it also holds true that the wrong method can sink your project to the bottom of the corporate ocean.

Letting people make their own decisions in an organization whose culture does not encourage such independence may leave you with indecisive team members or, even worse, decisions made solely on the basis of popularity and social acceptance rather than project needs. It may seem that more roads lead to Rome, but don't forget that it is actually a maze.

CHAPTER TWO

Project Potion

The people surrounding your project, the stakeholders, mainly determine the circumstances of the project. In Chapter 1, you learned that you need to cut and paste your own approach from existing methods and techniques, depending on these circumstances. That is easier said than done. But don't be scared, because the rest of this book covers the topic of stakeholders.

At the end of all those pages, you will feel like an alchemist that throws all kinds of liquids into a jar, mixing it up, stirring it, and creating the perfect blend, a kind of secret potion. At one time, you may need Project Potion No. 4, and on another occasion you may find yourself completely happy drinking Project Potion No. 1. I'm mentioning this just in case you are wondering why this chapter is called "Project Potion."

If I take Chapter 1 and mix it up with some project management lingo, you will get the following approach:

1. You analyze the stakeholders and their interests and expectations

2. You analyze the products (technical stuff) you have to create

3. You determine the potential risks that might exist

4. You create a project approach that reduces those risks; for this, you have three main tools:

   - *Strategy*: What are the steps taken in the project, and what is the sequence and time frame?

   - *Organization*: How is your project organization constructed?

   - *Feedback*: How is the feedback to the stakeholders on the status and content of products and process organized?

You as a software project manager are also a stakeholder of the project, and you also get feedback on the product and the process. Based on this feedback, you will be repeating these steps more than one time, to adapt your approach to the current situation.

Figure 2-1: Project Potion Approach

Again, here I am throwing in some project management lingo: step 1 would involve *stakeholder analysis*, and the other steps would be *risk management*. A project management model that clearly reflects the repetitive nature of project management activities is the *spiral model*.

The Spiral Model

After reading the section titled "One Size Doesn't Fit All" in Chapter 1, you might get the impression that the steps a project manager has to take might vary greatly. Although that is true, it doesn't mean there isn't more to say about it. In the same chapter, I mentioned the existence of a project management process, and this is exactly the spot that will bring some sanity to this matter. There is a process to define that holds true in all situations of software projects.

Barry W. Boehm and P. Bose[8] provide the software world with a spiral model that gives us an idea about the basic steps a project manager has to take. The interesting part of this model lies in the term "spiral." The steps a project manager has to take during a project are cyclic in nature; in other words, there is a set of activities you keep on repeating until your project is finished.

If you think about it for more than one second, it all makes sense. First you think about what goal you have to reach, next you decide what would be the best way to do this, and then you do it. After that, if you haven't finished your project yet, you plan your next steps, which start again with defining what goals you have to reach in the next cycle.

Or, to use the spiral model definition of it:

1. Determine the *objectives* you want to accomplish, the *alternatives* you might have to reach those objectives, and how *constraints* provide the borders of your operating area. With a special focus on stakeholders, you get the following steps:

   a. Identify stakeholders

   b. Identify stakeholders' interests and expectations (called *win conditions*)

   c. Reconcile these interests and expectations; negotiate objectives, constraints, and alternatives

2. Evaluate the product and process alternatives based upon the information gathered in the previous step. Identify the risks attached and resolve those risks.

3. Develop the product defined in Step 2 according to the process defined in the previous step.

Define the next level of product (the stuff you have to do next) and process, including partitions of them.

4. Plan the next phases by validating and reviewing the product and process definitions, and get commitment from the stakeholders.[8]

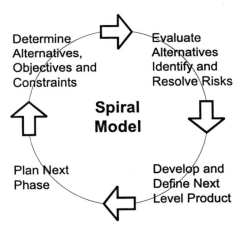

Figure 2-2: Barry W. Boehm and P. Bose's Spiral Model

This approach has some important aspects:

1. It allows you to have multiple cycles. This is important, as in this way different project strategies are supported. You can do a big design up front and then implement the plans or you can take a more incremental approach where you deliver parts of a system one at a time.

2. It explicitly takes into account the needs of
    stakeholders, supporting all aspects mentioned in
    the "Mindset of the Software Project Manager"
    section in Chapter 1.

3. It dictates that you make decisions about what to
    do next, so set priorities and evaluate
    alternatives. This may seem obvious; however,
    making *explicit* decisions about this is a part that
    is easily forgotten when a project is running for a
    while.

Risk Management

In previous sections I have discussed expectations,
estimations, and anticipations. I tried to make it sound as
good as possible, but let's face it, it's all vague stuff. You
have to think about how someone else thinks and base your
complete approach on that assessment. We will handle
requirements later on and state that it's best to assume that
they are wrong and will change anyway. It's like flipping a
coin or playing cards.

Software project management cannot be performed
without a good system to handle all these unknown parameters.
A project manager has to be able to live with uncertainties and
have a good way to structure the approach for handling them.
The first is a personal aspect that you have to do all by yourself.
The latter is where *risk management* comes in.

*Risk management focuses the project manager's
attention on those portions of the project most likely to*

cause trouble and to compromise participants' win conditions.[2]

So, in other words, it's a set of actions that helps the project manager structure his approach for dealing with the unknown or the things that are not certain. As Elaine M. Hall puts it:

> [...] we define risk as the possibility of loss. We obtain an instance of risk by specifying values for the risk attributes of probability (the possibility) and consequence (the loss). Probability is the likelihood that the consequence will occur. Consequence is the effect of an unsatisfactory outcome.[9]

So the idea is to specify explicitly the items that you are not sure about and define what will happen if what is expected (or assumed) is not true.

If you are not sure about the estimate ending of a certain task, you can define the risk for this situation as follows: delay of the actual end of the activity = very likely to happen.

The problem with risk management is the negative image associated with the word "risk." Of course, unless there is a potential for loss, there is no risk. The loss can be either a bad outcome or a lost opportunity. The tendency of most stakeholders is to jump very nervously at the statement, "This is a risk." Therefore, most of the time it's not very easy to discuss risks because that's always a conversation about problems. It's very important that the risk is not perceived as a bad thing but as a positive attitude to make sure everyone will become a winner in the end.

61

Remember, risk management helps you to be aware of the goals you have to achieve and what can happen if you don't satisfy the goals. It supports you in making the right choices. So risk is not a bad thing. Say it out loud! Spread the word!

Stakeholder Analysis

Stakeholder analysis is a technique to identify and analyze the stakeholders surrounding a project. It provides information on stakeholders and their relationships, interests, and expectations.

A proper analysis of the stakeholders will help you to construct a project approach suited to the situation and will allow you to negotiate better with the stakeholders.

This may all seem very misty and cloudy, but keep remembering why you must do it:

- Expectations are assessable and can be influenced. However, you should stay true to the interests of people; they will determine the amount of leverage you have to change the expectations without setting a stakeholder on the warpath.

- Requirements have to stay in line with what people are expecting. If stakeholders find out the requirements don't fit their expectations, you have a major problem.

- Knowledge about the stakeholders and their expectations and interests help you shape the project organization (on structure, authority, and responsibility).

- It's a very good risk analysis strategy to see where the potential problems will be.

Stakeholder analysis will help you to construct the organization and communication needed for your particular project and will provide you with a first set of risks.

Tailoring at Start-Up

Inherent to the spiral approach, and actually to all the concepts and assumptions in this book, is a determination not to be limited to any one way of managing a project. However, at some point you have to define this strategy. It is actually a part of every project management cycle in the spiral model.

Please don't make the mistake of doing this all by yourself. I know that it can be very tiresome to have "method discussions" at the start of a project, or even halfway through it. But lets face it, most people are familiar with more than one approach and you will certainly have these discussions anyway. By involving multiple participants in the decisions regarding what steps to take, you also eliminate an important potential project-killer, the *not-invented-here syndrome*.

Do you know the best way to frustrate a perfectly good process? Issue a directive. Tell the employees they must work in a certain way. You will see your well-oiled machinery fall victim to sabotage and come to a screeching, project-devastating halt. People are funny in this respect. When anything concerns their own work, they want something to say about it. They want to determine how they work. When introducing a project style of working to an organization, lack of employee involvement is one of the main causes of failure.

Some years ago, I experienced an organizational environment in which all projects were torpedoed by changing requirements. In an effort to get a grip on the situation, the project managers looked for techniques to control the situation. They found that they had everything they thought they needed in place; they had already installed every procedure that they could find in literature. And still the projects were sinking under the heavy burden of continuous change. Purely by accident, the project managers stumbled across a project team member at the coffee machine claiming, "The procedure was installed, but no one is actually using it. The project manager issued this procedure out of the blue, so it's his darn thing, not mine."

This phenomenon actually has a name: the not-invented-here syndrome. This tendency to refuse to accept something simply because it's not of your own making is very widespread, much more prevalent than you can imagine. Why am I telling you this at this moment? I'm doing so because a lot of introductions on managing projects are directives from above: "Starting next month, you will have to make a plan for every work activity you perform and you will have to record all the time you spend on tasks." And as I was saying when I began this section, that is a very good way to frustrate a process.

Related to this issue of employee acceptance is another argument in favor of letting the people involved in the work determine the way that work is done: who knows how to work better than the people performing the job?

The Scale-Up Method

If you put a couple of people together to create something, you can just leave them alone and let them do their stuff. Being the professionals they are, they might just surprise you with how good the results are. Project management techniques such as procedures are invented to avoid potential problems. If you don't have the problem, you don't need the cure.

You would be surprised to learn how many projects suffer from formal aspects that the team members follow just because a project is supposed to have them. If techniques are put into place without a potential problem to address, you have plain old bureaucracy. And that is another ideal way to cripple a project.

Barry W. Boehm and Richard Turner provide us with a perfect guideline about how much of the project process should be regulated: "Is it riskier for me to apply (more of) this process component or to refrain from applying it?" [7]

In other words, when putting a procedure into place, does it reduce a serious risk or does it only introduce worse problems? So you start out as simply as possible, and add process components one at a time, when they are actually needed. And when you introduce them, make sure you explain why this is being done.

Starting out with the basics and then scaling the method up when needed also makes it easier to introduce process components into a larger organization. For success, you should take it nice and easy and explain what risk it addresses.

Introducing Process Components to the Organization

Raising a child has its difficulties. You can say 42 times, "Don't run, you might fall," but actually having a little (harmless) fall makes a more lasting impression. This doesn't mean that the parent is better off throwing the kid onto the pavement. The parent tries to guide the child through the process of learning and experiencing. Just think, you get all this wisdom from someone who has no kids.

Now let's get back to the kids in the organization. Starting the different way of working at the individual employee level raises the critique that the employees are too stupid to change. You may hear, "They performed this job in this way for 30 years. These guys are too old to change" and more arguments like this one. I agree that simply instructing employees to deliver process descriptions that comply with a project approach doesn't work, but a little guidance in the activity works miracles.

66

This guidance should answer the big "why": why do we need a new process? Why should it look like this? You could provide everyone with this fabulous book. People should know why the game is played like this; that's the key to success.

To middle management who will assume the role of customer, visibility should be the mantra. Schedules, budgets, and results should be transparent. The project manager should clarify issues to avoid as many surprises as possible. That approach will probably sell itself. Of course, some discipline from the customer is required, and ambitious goals with no budget and a very narrow time frame will be killed from the start. In that case, the only thing about the project that becomes transparent is its impossibility. High visibility also makes it difficult to change your mind and pretend you haven't. Certainly middle management can change initial tactics at some point, but it's 100% clear that changes are taking place. When your original strategy has been made so public, you can hardly claim later that you are following the same old path when you so obviously have changed routes. This can be a drawback for managers.

When dealing with technical employees such as programmers, the trick is to show them that better planning is more relaxed. For example, if programmers can provide the project manager with a reliable estimate of how long they need for a certain job, they can do their work at their own pace without time schedules slipping and pressures building (assuming the project manager doesn't slash every estimate by 50%). When this relationship between realistic estimates and working conditions is clear, just show employees the way to improve their ability to plan. Watts S. Humphrey[10] has constructed a complete process for doing this. The essence is to let people record what they are doing and how long it takes, so they can see for themselves which tasks consume the most time and take action to improve efficiency. This method makes visible how long a certain task actually takes. When asked for an estimate, workers can then make more informed guesses based upon their records of previous tasks, such as "System X cost me one month. This system has a little more functionality, so I would estimate completion time as two months."

So filling in timesheets is the way to go? If you put it like that, no, it's not. Just read the previous paragraph again and compare its employee-centered method with the use of timesheets to control the programmers in a directive manner. With approaches such as "You are late! Why?" or "This takes too long! Why?" you will be heading for a sure disaster.

What Makes Your Project a True Project?

Your company tries to accomplish something by tackling a project; it is not taking on a project just for the heck of it. Sometimes it seems that there is no apparent reason, but normally some business objectives are behind the goal of the project: beat the competition by offering a new service, reduce costs by streamlining the working process, and so forth. There must be something behind the whole endeavor.

The business objectives and the priorities are of great importance in determining how you will end up doing the project. If it's speed that you need, you will possibly take some shortcuts, and if it is quality you are after, the system may never be down (for example, you may build some extra safety measures into your project process). It is important to know up front the goals of the project, and that is what this section is all about. First, though, you have to make sure that what you are going to do actually *is* a project.

For All the Right Reasons

Managing projects is hip. At least, that's the impression you might get, considering the number of projects and project managers all around. It's not that surprising when you keep in mind that our ever-changing world asks for activities with continually increasing complexity. We have to keep reinventing the way we do things. We invent it and then we throw it away, because thanks to rampant obsolescence, what works well one time is often useless a second time. It's an environment governed by survival of the fittest projects. .

By definition, a *project* is a temporary activity with a starting date, specific goals and conditions, defined responsibilities, a budget, a planning strategy, a fixed end date, and the involvement of multiple parties. You know what you have to do, you do it once, and that's the end of it: that's a project. However, being hip has its disadvantages. Our local housing office has a permanent project manager for financial controlling. This is an ongoing activity for the office, and the project manager does it as his full-time, never-ending job. Whatever he's managing, it surely ain't a project.

There is no real harm in naming a tiger an elephant or vice versa. No one is harmed by calling a job a project, even if it misses fitting the definition by a mile. But don't be surprised if techniques for projects don't work on projects in name only. Don't be amazed if applying the techniques may seem like killing a bumblebee with a machine gun. And don't get mad when other people don't know why you're doing an easy job the hard way by making a project out of it.

Start a project, but only for the right reasons, and not for the heck of it, or because of the cool title or the status.

Look for the following aspects:

- Starting date

- Specific goals and conditions

- Defined responsibilities

- Budget

- Planning

- Fixed end date

- Multiple parties involved

And then, if it looks like a duck, walks like a duck, and quacks like a duck, it probably is a duck. However, if it doesn't come close, questioning whether to treat it like a project is the right thing to do. There may be a quicker and much simpler solution. Olivier D'Herbemont and Bruno Cesar see the inflation of problems into so-called "projects" as having broad-ranging consequences:

> Often [...] top management has no project; it merely has a problem and does not know how to, or does not want to, find a solution. So, it expects the players to find the way. Much social and industrial unrest can be caused by top management not having real projects but only having the desire to get rid of a problem.[11]

If you don't find all the aspects named above at this moment in time, it is still possible that you are dealing with a project. Wait a bit, and make the final judgment at the end of the intake. Working on one of the subjects might cause one of the aspects to pop up.

Determining Cause and Goal

There is a meaning to life. If you have a religious or scientific point of view, it's clear there is a direction we're all headed in and some purpose to what we do. And that's nice. The days of doing something just because someone told us to do so are over, I hope.

All activities should have a goal to support and, even better, a goal that is seen as useful and attainable. Digging a hole so that another poor fool can fill it again is an attainable goal, but it fails the other criterion of usefulness. You may laugh at this and wave it away as trivial and a far stretch from reality. You poor soul, you are probably not long out of reality back here in the asylum.

71

Projects, being a collection of activities, have goals. These goals should be the answer to every "'why" question about the project. Reviewing several projects, you will probably find some statements about the goals to be achieved. I'm sure, however, that searching for information about the reason for the project will yield less data. And it's the reason that provides you with some hint about the usefulness of the goals. It can give insight on dependencies with other projects so you can avoid having another project fill the hole you just dug.

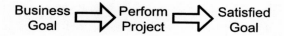

Figure 2-3: Every Project Should Have a Goal to Accomplish

The following questions may give you a start in your search for the answer to the big "why" question:

- What strategic decision led to this project?

- How does this project relate to the business plan?

- Is this project the follow-up to another project?

- What will be done with the results of this project?

- What will happen if this project is canceled?

- Is this project related to other projects that take place in the same time frame?

- Does the competition address the same issues taken on by this project?

- Why was such a project not performed earlier?

Determining Scope

The happy couple decided not to make a fuss about their wedding. It would be a very small event for a few special friends. After a visit to the girl's mother, it became two small events: one ceremony at City Hall and one at the local church. By the time the couple took leave of the groom's mother, all elderly aunts had been invited and, as they were all of very advanced age, every one of them would be staying over on the night of the festivities. The day she spoke with her best friend, the bride simply had to have this fabulous designer dress, one that would require three bridesmaids to carry the train.

Does this sound familiar? You don't have to plan a wedding to witness firsthand the spectacle of something starting out elegant and simple and then snowballing into nightmarish proportions. You've probably heard stories of people who set out just to fix a dripping shower and ended up completely remodeling their bathrooms. You must know when to stop and then just simply stop.

With a software project, it is essential to know the boundaries up front. Which aspects are allowed, and which ones are off-limits? If the goal is to cut costs, why not just fire everyone? You could imagine that these kinds of changes in personnel are not within the scope of a project.

However, switching to a different technology would be within the project's boundaries. You are allowed to change internal procedures, but not the interfaces with external parties. The scope can contain all kinds of statements, and the trick is to get it as detailed as possible at this early stage. Together with the goal and the constraints, the scope provides information about the leeway you have in this project.

The scope can be too large to fit in a certain time frame or too small to satisfy the goal. In determining the scope, you talk with the concerned parties and ask two types of questions:

- Can we change this?

- Must we change this?

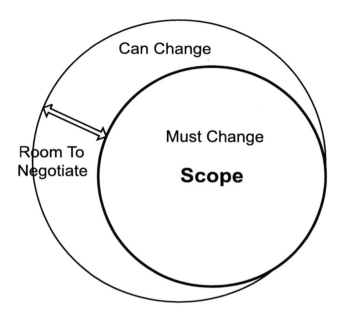

Figure 2-4: Scope--What Must Be Changed and What Can Be Changed?

You should take advantage of what you *can* change by using it as ammunition to get the needed win-win situations that enable you to handle what *must* be changed. Wow, play that sentence again, Sam.

Suppose you are allowed to change the scope of training sessions but do not have to do so. Then imagine that you must change the way a certain department works, so that administrative procedures now done manually can be totally automated. Employees might be understandably reluctant to become little more than typing goats. By providing extra training to make workers more state-of-the-art in their field and emphasizing that automation will free up time for them to handle more challenging tasks, you might create the win-win situation you need. In this way, you should hammer out a scope that fits the goals, constraints, and expectations of the stakeholders. To prevent a visit from your dear old aunts, send them a piece of the wedding cake instead!

CHAPTER THREE

Stakeholder Analysis

Suppose you've been doing the same job for over twenty years. You work every day of your life with the system's five screens, you really know every little pixel of these screens, and it is your digital empire. All of a sudden after all those years, a big shot walks in and tells you that everything is about to change. There will soon be a new system, and it's up to you to tell the technicians what they should construct.

But after all those years, your business world consists of the ten options you have in your input fields. You actually see your business process only in terms of pixels, and you realize this. You are painfully aware of the fact that you cannot think outside the box, and you suspect that management just might find out that you are not competent to perform your current job. They won't learn that right now because you know all the tricks in the present system, but when a new system replaces that one, you will be a sitting duck. Chances are that when the guys in the suits come to talk about what the new system should do, you will do little more than describe and explain the old system, because your requirement for the user interface is that everything should be the same. You have done this job for twenty years, so you should know.

An alert project manager would help you out by providing you with the proper training and support to actually perform the job using the new system. He would have discovered that although you are worried about the changes, you would welcome the chance to try new and exciting things if you felt more secure about your future. .

How would the project manager know all this? He would perform a proper stakeholder analysis.

The steps for a stakeholder analysis are:

- Stakeholder identification
  Who are the stakeholders?

- Stakeholder expectations and interests
  What are the expectations and the interests of the stakeholders?

- Stakeholder influence and role in the project
  How should they be involved in the project to have the best possible outcome?

Stakeholder Identification

Think about your project as a Shakespearean tragedy.
Visualize it as a play with all your stakeholders on a stage
clad in tights and big, floppy hats and speaking in this weird
language. "Wilt thou be gone? It is not yet near day." It
helps you to put things into perspective, and it will not be
that far from reality.

During the project intake, the software project
manager should create a mental picture of who the
stakeholders are. Before the play can start, you should at
least know your cast. Olivier D'Herbemont and Bruno César
call it "the field of play":

> In theory, nothing is simpler than to draw up the field
> of play for a project. It defines itself. [. . .] A new
> information system is to be introduced? The players
> are the computer suppliers and the users. [. . .]
> However, defining the field of play always throws up
> surprises. One starts by working very calmly on a clean
> sheet of paper on a flip-chart . Soon there are ten
> sheets stuck to the wall of the meeting room, each
> filled with arrows, crosses and question marks. At the
> end of the day, there are still unanswered questions.[11]

So, what you basically do is to stand in front of a white
board and start drawing relationships between parties and
people, indicating why they are stakeholders in the project.

The field of play consists of groups and individuals.
However, when we talk about demands, only individuals
should be considered. When it seems like a group makes any

79

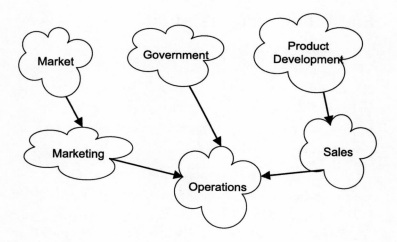

Figure 3-1: A Sample Field of Play

demands or indicates other kinds of properties normally associated with individuals, you have to look for a leader of the group, a representative, and substitute this person for the group. It is not a group that has dreams or wishes; it is a person.

When listing stakeholders or creating groups, there are two approaches: (1) considering the stakeholders based upon their normal role within the company or associated companies (for example, departments or third-party suppliers); and (2) considering the stakeholders based upon their intended role within the project (for example, tester, developer, user representative, architect).

Sample Stakeholders by "Normal Role"	Sample Stakeholders by "Project Role"
• Sales	• Project Manager
• Marketing	• Customer
• Financial Department	• Developer
• Controlling	• Architect
• Debtor Administration	• Database Administrator
• Production	• User
• Product Development	• Tester
• Human Resources	
• IT Department	
• Software Vendor	
• Government	

Stakeholder Expectations

You have a map of all your stakeholders, you know who they are, and you know why you should consider them as stakeholders. The next step is to get some input on their expectations. We can ask them flat out what these are and throw in some other questions to provide us with some useful extra information. You can send these inquiries by e-mail and ask that the responses be returned by e-mail. Especially when the number of stakeholders is large, it's a very nice, convenient method.

You should include the following questions:

1. What are your expectations of the project?
    Just phrase the question as boldly as you can.

2. What is the purpose or mission of the project team?
    This Indicates what the stakeholder thinks is the goal of the project.

3. What benefits are there likely to be?
    What does the stakeholder have to gain from the project?

81

4. What are your top priorities?
   Are there any conflicts with other issues? How important is the project for this stakeholder?

5. What resources are you willing to commit/ reluctant to commit?
   This indicates the level of commitment and participation.

6. Do you expect some conflict of interest?
   Has the stakeholder something to lose in the project?

7. How do you regard other stakeholders on the list?
   Can you expect some struggles between certain stakeholders?

8. What outcome is needed and/or expected from the project?
   This gives you explicit expectations about the project results.

9. When should the team's work be completed? What milestones do you expect?
   This gives you explicit expectations about project process.

10. To whom does the team report and how often?
    Who's calling the shots? Look for the real hierarchy.

11. What is the business case for the project?
    This indicates the expectations for the business.

12. What organizational policies influence the project?
    Policies can be regarded as expectations of the organization.

13. What are your experiences with similar projects (personally and/or departmentally)?
    History determines one's current expectations.

Stakeholder Interests

As stated before, the stakeholder interests are the Holy Grail, the stuff you are really looking for. No one will make things easy by simply telling you them, so these are the aspects you just have to "guesstimate." In an attempt to bring some structure to this largely unmapped territory, I present the following checklist to assist in the analysis. Remember, this is just a short sample list to give you an idea and a starting point. It is in no way complete.

I use three groups of needs (interests): personal, relatedness, and growth. They are taken from Clayton P. Alderfer,[12] a psychologist who studied the needs of people in general. I could also have borrowed from other sources, but this one seems to fit best.

Personal

- Work Orientation versus Family Orientation
  Is the person more focused on the work environment or the home front?

- Satisfaction with Current Job
  Important to know when creating a job description. If not satisfied, perhaps include some new, more exciting content to the job.

- Satisfaction with Current Organization
  A broader aspect than "satisfaction with job": do you need to be aware of some resentment a person might have against the organization?

- Desire to Gain More Skill/Knowledge in a Certain Area
  Giving someone the opportunity to improve competency in a certain area is a great motivator.

- Sufficient Appreciation
  Showing some appreciation can boost a person's performance.

- Reduction/Expansion of Workload
  Does someone want to do more or less? As a project manager, you don't always have the authority to influence this, but you might give it a shot.

- Reduction/Expansion of Responsibility
  Actually, comments are the same as above.

- Infection by Not-Invented-Here Syndrome
  Does someone have a great need to be involved in something to accept it? If yes, and you need the person, then ensure involvement.

Relatedness (Interpersonal/Social)

- Recognition of Knowledge Among Peers
  Outside the Organization
  If someone has a strong need for recognition
  among his or her own peers, try to incorporate it
  into the job. See also "Reference Group" later in
  this chapter.

- Recognition of Job Competence within the
  Organization (Hierarchy)
  *Does the person feel his or her work goes
  unnoticed in the organization? Does the person
  want to keep a higher profile?*

- Covering Up Own Incompetence (Don't Rock
  the Boat)
  *Some people try to maintain a low profile and
  avoid attracting any attention to themselves to
  cover up some incompetence.*

- Boosting Another's Reputation (Sponsorship)
  *It is nice to get some insight into who is friends
  with whom and who works to give others a good
  reputation. Sponsors can work nicely together,
  but be skeptical about the judgments made about
  each other.*

- Undermining Another's Reputation
  *Actually, the opposite of the above situation:
  who is trashing whom? Try to avoid putting
  these antagonists   together.*

- Attempt to Move to Another Job within the Organization
  Will not do much about own job or assignment, but can be found meddling in the desired area where he or she has no authority.

- Attempt to Build an Empire within the Organization
  Very dynamic personality and worth soliciting for maximum influence in the project, if only for sheer number of personal connections.

- Attempt to Maintain an Empire within the Organization
  Looks the same as person mentioned above, but has a more defensive attitude and will try to avoid as much change as possible.

- Attempt to Increase Sphere of Influence within Organization
  This person makes assignments bigger than they actually are.

Existence (Material Interests)

- Desire for More Money
  Need I say more?

- Desire for More Tools
  Any questions?

- Desire for a Bigger Office
  Look for a real-estate agent.

What Drives Project People?

It's difficult to really put your finger on the subject of stakeholder interests. It is more a guessing game than a science, so we need to make as much sense of the topic as we can. I conducted a small study on visitors to my website who work on software projects, in an effort to gain some insight into what actually drives project people.

From the results, I came up with five aspects that affected almost 80% of the responses. Read them, and when analyzing a particular stakeholder, try to see in what way each of these aspects affects that person.

The five aspects that drive project people are:

1. Process versus. Content

2. Reference Group

3. Change versus. Status Quo

4. Defined versus Creative

5. Group versus Individual

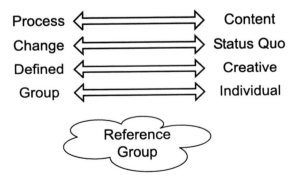

Figure 3-2: What Drives Project People?

1. Process versus Content

A big difference among stakeholders involved in your project is their preference for either the process or the content. Taking this distinction to its extreme, consider a senior manager who gets his thrills by changing the entire organization, and then think about the programmer who lights up when discussing network protocols.

Process fetishists can generally be found working at higher levels of the organization. They are into the "game" of projects, and it's the journey that they most enjoy. Content lovers, on the other hand, can be found at the more operational levels, most of the time constituting the people actually in your project team. It's not as much the journey as the destination they get their kicks from. Project managers tend to have a mix of both flavors, but of course this is a generalization.

Knowing what tendency people have towards either process or content provides you with some great leads on how to motivate them. For example, a strong preference for content makes it important to know the goals of the project. What will be the end result, and why? Simply letting project team members in on these questions has an amazing effect on their motivation.

2. Reference Group

Another aspect to consider is the group of people the stakeholders measure themselves against, or their reference group. Software engineers tend to compare themselves with other software engineers, not only within their own company but also in a wider range, even internationally. Management members mostly compare themselves with other people within their companies' hierarchies.

Stakeholders use the reference group to formulate their own interests: "I want to earn as much as Big Shot Shirley." "I want to be as good as Leisure Suit Lenny." "I want to have more power than Head Honcho Harry." If you know with whom stakeholders compare themselves, you have an important piece of information to build incentives or at least to know what drives the stakeholders.

3. Change versus Status Quo

Projects are always about change, and the real project die-hards embrace ever-changing environments. If you operate in larger companies, however, you will most likely have members on your project team that are not change lovers—people who feel more secure with the things they know, with things just as they are now.

4. Defined versus Creative

How many times did you think that you had everything covered by putting a perfect procedure into place, only to find out that you were the only one sticking to the procedure? Putting a structure into place may be a good thing for one person but a real motivation-killer for another. "This rigid structure is ruining my creativity!" You must have heard that one before.

You should steer with the right amount of defined processes. Stuffing a large binder with procedures, committees, and formats to follow is definitely a sure way to make some good people very unhappy.

And then there are the guys and gals that love a fixed plan. Most of the time, they are also the ones who dislike change.

5. Group versus Individual

Consider the lone wolf that hacks away at programming code in the dead of night. Put him in a nine-to-five regimen in an exposed office environment and watch his productivity plummet. The other way around, put me all by myself without any social contacts, and you can see me dying a slow and lonely death. If people love to operate alone, don't force them to be social just for the sake of team spirit. Preference for working in a group or working as an individual is an important factor that a project manager can use to motivate the project people.

Sociodynamics

Olivier D'Herbemont and Bruno César have another way of looking at stakeholders surrounding a project. Their approach is best suited for a project conducted in a highly political environment and is called Sociodynamics. The main feature of Sociodynamics is that you map people according to two aspects:

1. The amount of energy they are dedicating in favor of the project

2. The amount of energy they are dedicating against the project[11]

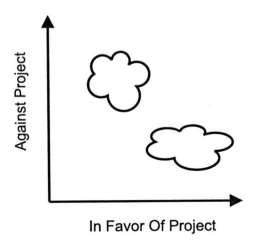

Figure 3-3: Sociodynamics—Are You For or Against the Project?

At first, it might seem a little strange to consider people in respect to those two dimensions: you are either for or against, friend or foe, right? Well, not entirely. The most useful stakeholders have a strong commitment to the project but are not unreasonably fanatical about it. They have a specific level of skepticism and provide you with great insights. They don't unquestioningly follow orders but will raise their voices when they have doubts. Exactly what you need! Well, yes, if you want to succeed. You don't want people who think everything is dandy and just blindly follow the plan. At least, you don't want that type of stakeholder everywhere.

Stakeholders who are perpetually against the project can be a pain in the butt too. To handle this type of person, D'Herbemont and César provide us with great advice: focus on your allies. If you have to get some points across and people are opposed to your position, the natural reaction is to try to win them over by paying a lot of attention to them. Instead, you should align yourself with those who agree with you and support them in their efforts to convince the opponents. This way, you have more people to spread the word, mostly from the same environment as the I-don't-wanna's. And we all share the tendency to accept something more readily from someone out of the same environment than from a total stranger.

Stakeholder Influence and Its Role in a Project

What does all this analyzing and guessing bring to us at the end of this chapter? That's a good question, and here's the answer:.

1. A list of all the stakeholders

2. An idea about each stakeholder's relative importance and influence

3. Insight into what stakeholders want out of the project

4. Insight into what makes stakeholders tick

5. An idea about whether stakeholders will work against or for the project

These insights about the stakeholders will be needed later on (Chapter 5) to help us construct the *project organization*:

- Do we have to include the stakeholders in the organization?

- If so, is it wise to grant stakeholders great influence or should we give them positions where they can do no harm?

- How can we construct stakeholders' job descriptions in such a way that they are as motivated as possible?

The feedback that we discuss in a very large part of this book also benefits from a stakeholder analysis. For all the aspects considered important to the stakeholders, you have to make sure a good feedback mechanism is put into place to avoid having stakeholders going on some kind of a rampage.

CHAPTER FOUR

Risk Management

There will be a lot of things in and around your project that you don't know. Uncertainties are a fact of project life. How long will the project really take? Will the user requirements change? How will the system perform using a certain infrastructure? These and many other questions can make a project manager nervous.

You shouldn't be nervous. You should just be prepared. And that's where risk management comes in.

Risk Assessment

What you don't know can't hurt you. Yeah, sure, right . . . *not!* When you are hooked on cigarettes and smoking like a maniac, chances are that you will claim you aren't addicted.

Even if you can't stop, there's always that classic defensive response, "If I really wanted to stop, I could do it right now." You are in denial. You know you have a problem, but you're not mentally ready to accept it. In projects, you also have these kinds of denial issues. You know problems can occur, but you just ignore the whole matter, hoping that troubles will never appear or that, if they do, they will just blow over like a harmless gust of wind, never to be seen again. After all, you don't want to rock the boat . . . you can cross that bridge when you come to it . . . there's no problem that can't be solved by hard work. There are lots of perfectly good clichés that encourage you to ignore potential risks.

So basically, there are things that you know you don't know. Ignoring them is bad, but at least you know that these problems are lurking out there somewhere. And yep, there are even more problematic possibilities, in the form of stuff you don't even realize you don't know. These are the problems that will sneak up on you, and you'll never know what hit you. It's very difficult to prepare yourself for what is truly unknown.

After you have handled this risk business for years, you develop a nose for it. You have feelings (♬ *FEELINGS, hohoho, FEELINGS, lalala* ♬). These are mostly of the intuitive kinds called "gut feelings." But how do you develop this ability to identify risks? In other words, how do you bootstrap your gut? The answer, my friend, is . . . checklists. Start creating lists of points that you want to review for risks. As you do this more often, your checklists will grow, and you can put the results of all your experiences in them to avoid the problems in the future. How should you get started? First of all, remember that you are not alone, and this is not a unique situation you are in. So, of course, there are standard checklists you can use to get you on your way. The Software Engineering Institute (www.sei.cmu.edu) provides a very nice starting point. Its risk taxonomy is a structured checklist that organizes software development risks into a certain framework.

The software taxonomy is organized into three major classes:

1. **Product Engineering:** the technical aspects of the work to be accomplished

2. **Development Environment:** the methods, procedures, and tools used to produce the product

3. **Program Constraints:** the contractual, organizational, and operational factors within which the software is developed but which are generally outside of the direct control of the local management[13]

As described by Marvin J. Carr et al., these taxonomic classes are further divided into elements and each element is characterized by its attributes.[14]

However, a list itself is not very practical. The Software Engineering Institute also provides an associated questionnaire for free. For every attribute of the list, there is an associated question to make things more explicit and easier to answer.

These questions take the form of the following sample:

Are there any problems with performance?

- Throughput

- Scheduling asynchronous real-time events

- Real-time response

- Recovery timelines

- Response time

- Database response, contention, or access[13]

By going through all the questions, you are forced to think about almost every aspect of your software project to see if there is an underlying uncertainty.

Using the checklist method along with all the other information in this book, you will come a long way. The following sample checklist could be named "Stakeholders' Risk Taxonomy" or, more appropriately, simply "My List." I created it by spending thirty minutes writing down some aspects I covered in the previous chapters. It is not intended to be complete but is merely given as an example of how you can construct a checklist based on ideas from this book.

Writing It Down

In the previous section, we talked about how to start considering the risks. You take a certain aspect and think about it in terms of what you don't know or what might go

Stakeholders		
		• Have you identified all stakeholders? • Have you identified the leader or spokesperson from each group? • Have you ever met the stakeholders? • Do you have information on the background of the stakeholders (history)?

Stakes		
	Fears	• Do you know what the fears generally are for each type of stakeholder you have (for example, programmers)? • Do you know what the fears of the stakeholders are per group? • Do you know what the fears for each individual are? • Do you know how this project affects the fears of the stakeholders?
	Wishes	• Do you know what the wishes generally are for each type of stakeholder you have (for example, programmers)? • Do you know what the wishes of the stakeholders are per group? • Do you know what the wishes are for each individual? • Do you know how this project affects the wishes of the stakeholders?

Requirements		
	Product	• Are the cause and goal of the project clear to you? • Is the project scope identified and does it include what you can change, what you must change, and what you can't change?
	Process	• Are the constraints identified (money, time, people)? • Do you have any idea how much room there is to negotiate these constraints? • If there are already estimates, do you know how much you can trust them? • Is the project strategy clear and easy? • Is the project organization identified? Does every member bring added value to the project?

Project Management		
		• Are you able to negotiate? • Are you able to think in terms of win-win situations? • Are you risk-averse? • Did you include your own stakes in the process? • Are you able to give the project back in case it smells like a trap?

Feedback		
		• Is everyone aware of the need for and use of giving feedback? • Have you any idea how to provide feedback? • Do you really understand the techniques you want to use? • Did you schedule time/money/people/activities to provide the feedback?

differently than expected. Even better, you do this exercise with some colleagues in a meeting. For every risk that you might come up with, you have to specify the following items:

- *Risk:* a description of the actual risk (example: uncertainty regarding availability of programming resources)

- *Impact or consequence:* the impact on the project (process or product) if the risk occurs (example: delay in construction interfaces)

- *Possibility:* the possibility that the risk will occur, using range such as high/medium/low (example: medium)

- *Action:* the action that can/will be taken to avoid the risk, reduce the chances of its happening, or reduce its impact (example: get planning clear or investigate possibility of external programmers)

- *Cost:* what it will cost in time or money if the risk occurs (example: delay of three weeks)

You have to periodically review the list that is generated in this way (once a week). If the list is too extensive to let you give all the risks your attention, you have to create some priorities. A nice way to do this is by creating a "top ten" list of the most urgent risks every time you construct a checklist, so you will be sure that you focus on the more important issues.

There are a lot more things to say about the subject of risk management, but first and foremost is a reminder that it is really a state of mind. And with the few things shown in this section, you have a good starting point to reach that state. Remember, risk is not a bad thing, and if you come up with an action to resolve it, then be sure to execute it. Don't just talk the talk but also walk the risk management walk.

Tailoring the Approach

You analyzed all the stakeholders and dived into the unknown of the project with risk management. And perhaps you are still wondering: what is the use? I will make that clear in this chapter, as it covers the subject of turning all that knowledge into a suitable project approach. You will use the business priorities and the uncertainties you discovered with a risk assessment to tailor the project *strategy* (using terms like *increments, iterations*, and *phases*) and the types of *feedback* you need to include.

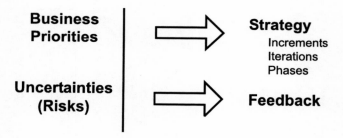

Figure 5-1: Impact of Business Priorities and Risks on the Project Approach

The insight you gain from using stakeholder analysis provides you with valuable angles to adapt the project *organization* (by stakeholder involvement and definition of the jobs and places in the project organization) and, again, the feedback you will need on the process and the product.

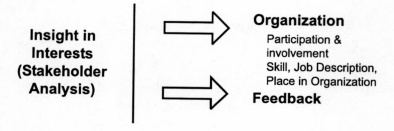

Figure 5-2: Impact of Stakeholder Interests on the Project Approach

Project Strategy

We have to decide what strategy the project should utilize. What kind of steps? In what sequence? With whom? I'm not talking about a fully detailed description: "George will walk to the bathroom. George will pull down his trousers." I'm talking about real strategy!

The traditional steps within a software project are something like this:

- We think about the subject

- We specify a solution for the subject

- We implement the solution

- We activate the solution in the organization

In project management lingo, we call these steps *phases* and have cool names for them like *analysis, specification, implementation,* and *rollout.*

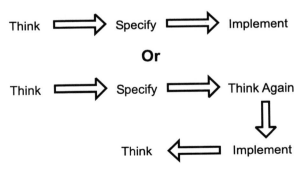

Figure 5-3: A Project Strategy Can Take Different Steps

At this moment you have to determine the phases, or major steps, that you will take. A strategy would be to follow the steps as mentioned above (the traditional one). You could do this if what has to be done is absolutely clear and everyone agrees. If not, this is not the way to go. When the time comes to implement the steps, what has been written in the specifications is no longer valid because people have changed their minds. Because this is often the case, a more common strategy is to repeat these steps (or some of them) several times. So, for example, instead of spending six months considering a subject and setting specifications for the whole year, a manager will handle the project through repeated cycles of spending two weeks thinking about the subject and writing specifications for four weeks. With every successive reiteration, the specifications get more and more detailed, and with each subsequent step you benefit from the results of previous steps.

The project strategy, like any other strategy, should be simple and logical; you must be able to explain it to someone unrelated to the project in two minutes. So don't go rushing into methods and use a lot of technical words like incremental, spiral, tornado, or waterfall. It only serves as camouflage for instances when you have no idea what you're talking about. If the goal is very unclear and the scope is totally undefined, the strategy will be too, so be sure to follow these steps in sequence:

- Set a clearly-defined goal

- Determine the scope

- Adjust the project according to the outcome of the previous step

- Execute the remainder of the project

It's okay to have the later steps more general than the first ones. It is a very simple strategy, but you can explain it to everyone, and it makes sense. If you don't know exactly what to do, your first job is to get that clear in your mind. The strategy should be a result of integrating all the information about the stakeholders you have collected.

Consider the following situation. The head of a user group has a formal role in determining the requirements for the product. You and some other people fear that these requirements will go beyond the scope of the project, but intervening continuously with the user chief may be considered as a threat to his independence or formal status. By creating some periodic steps for reviewing the requirements in relation to the scope with the concerned stakeholders, this problem can be overcome and you can achieve the desired win-win situation. The decision to set up these review steps, as in this sample case, is also an important part in determining the project strategy.

Uncertainties and Priorities

Discussing the project strategy is actually a game of looking at uncertainties, defining priorities, and making trade-offs among all of them.

From onset through completion of a project, there will be a lot of things that you don't know. What exactly do the users want? How well will the system perform? Will all personnel stay until the end of the project?

Alistair Cockburn (cited in Kevin Aguanno[15]) distinguishes three types of project uncertainties:

- *Predictable:* We don't know exactly what should be done or what the outcome will be, but the process to get it clear is quite straightforward. Unclear user requirements can be put on the table by using requirement determination steps.

- *Unpredictable, but resolvable:* The future is unclear, and the specified steps make it clear that it is not a simple, sequential process; however, we have a lot of techniques and options up our sleeves for tackling problems if they occur. An example is the performance of a complex of several systems. You can almost never predict how the systems will perform when every component is finally put into place, but when faced with potential problems, there are several technical solutions you can apply.

108

- *Unresolvable:* These are totally unknown factors and there is no way you will have possible solutions already at hand. Think, for example, about new regulations that the government might impose on your organization.

You have two proactive solutions to deal with uncertainties (a third passive one being to ignore them):

1. Make them clear as fast and early as possible by spending project resources to get information

2. Make sure your solution and project structure has the flexibility to cope with the uncertainties when they pop up

Both approaches will cost money. Cockburn coins the phrases *"money-for-information"* and *"money-for-flexibility"* for the two propositions (qtd. in Kevin Aguanno[15]).

Of equal importance to the uncertainties are the *business priorities* that have an influence on the choice of a good strategy. Based upon Barry W. Boehm and Richard Turner, they are:

- The *quality* of the solution that is required: an administrative system requires a different level of quality than the control system of a nuclear power plant

- The *scalability* of the solution that is required: is it something that is built once and perhaps has some small changes afterwards, or is it something that needs to grow bigger and bigger over an extended time frame?

- The *speed* at which the results are required: how fast should some sort of product be available in operation?[7]

Definitions and Strategies

Before we address the subject of choosing a strategy, we need to define some terms. The following definitions are taken from Pascal Van Cauwenberghe (cited in Kevin Aguanno):

> **A Phase:** A period in which some clearly defined task is performed. Just imagine that we require the following phases: Analysis, Design, Coding, Testing, Integration, and Deployment. Each phase has some inputs and some outputs.
>
> **To Iterate:** To perform some task in multiple passes. Each pass improves the result, until the result is 'finished.' Also called *rework*.
>
> **An Iteration:** A period in which a number of predefined tasks are performed. The results are evaluated to feed back to the next iteration.
>
> **An Increment:** A period in which some functionality is completed to a production-quality level.

A Release: Some coherent set of completed functionalities that is useful and usable to the intended users of the system.[15]

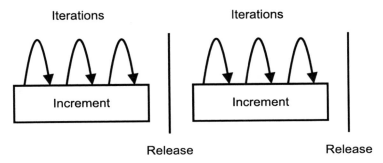

Figure 5-4: Releases, Increments, and Iterations

Using iterations, the users will get the system in each release in its entirety; all functions are more or less implemented. The users will provide feedback to the release and in the next iteration the functions are enhanced, corrected, or just changed. In this way, the system will evolve with each iteration.

If you are going to use increments, with each release the users will get one part of the system in its whole. Every time an increment is issued, they will get a new subsystem, or set of functionalities, added to the system they already have from the previous increments.

An increment is used to solve time issues by allowing you to bring a part of a system to production as quickly as possible, without having to wait until other subsystems are complete. Iterations are great for getting feedback as fast as possible. So if certain things are unclear, using iterations will make them clearer over time.

With increments and iterations, you are not limited to doing either one or the other; you can certainly mix and match them. For example, while developing a certain increment, you can use several iterations in the development process. You should also keep in mind that you can use these techniques not only on software but also on every product the project creates, like designs and requirement specifications.

When looking at applied strategies, you have at one extreme the traditional waterfall model with one iteration and one increment, which allows you to do everything in one go. At the other extreme you have more agile concepts that use numerous increments and iterations, providing you with some results as fast as possible and taking into account all uncertainties and possible changes.

The first draft of your strategy should be based on two mechanisms:

1. Defining iterations to get feedback to cover uncertainties (verification for quality or better scalability and verification as a feedback mechanism)

2. Defining increments that satisfy the business needs for speed

Project Organization

Darwin's natural selection is a great thing. The shape of
every species is crafted over thousands of years to optimize
the functions it needs to survive in its environment. If a
living thing does not have the necessary skills, it just dies
out and is doomed to extinction. All the beautiful, blonde,
long-legged creatures survive. The Homo Projectus,
however, is an ugly thing. It struggles to survive in extreme
situations where dirt has to be shoveled. In this respect, it
assumes the aspects of a lowly hog. Certain features are
required to ensure that the hogs will work together in such a
way that the pack will survive, and this is the tricky part. We
cannot simply wait until nature has killed off all unsuccessful
project organizations (the hog parties), so the software
project manager must give nature a little help, tinkering with
the organization so it might have a chance to survive in the
corporate jungle.

A project organization is a temporary thing; it will
only exist from the project's start until its end. All the
project team members come from different organizations or
different parts of one organization, and they will each have a
temporary assignment for the duration of the project. So
every project member has not only a project boss (the project
manager, perhaps you) but also a regular boss who issues
orders and assignments when the employee is not involved in
the project. These regular bosses represent an important
group of stakeholders. The project organization should be
developed from the project strategy, and it should be
constructed in such a way that the strategy can be

implemented within the environment of the project (look what the cat dragged in: a presumptuous sentence). Here's a very obvious example: if the strategy contains the feature of independent reviews, then the organization should support its independence by creating a separate working group with no ties to the other team members. But I'm getting a little ahead of myself now by mentioning working groups and the like.

The project team that does the work should be as small as possible. Small is beautiful, and effective. Don't start inviting everyone into the organization. Only people who have an added value and will devote a significant amount of time to the project can be in the core organization. Try to avoid going overboard on working groups. Working groups can drown a project in communication overhead. Besides, if there's still that much discussion, you should postpone the project until more decisions have been made.

While some of the people actually perform the work, others do nothing yet have some influence over the project. A large number of stakeholders fall into this category. The project organization can be used to satisfy some wishes of stakeholders to create the much-needed win-win situation. In its simplest form, this strategy can be applied by creating a project trashcan (The Project Tactical Non-Binding Advisory Committee, for instance) where you can deposit all the people you have no use for, the ones who want to be involved somehow just to retain control of their territories.

Be creative while shaping the project organization. Borrow from the Bob Ross artistic style to paint your organization: "This is a sweet little project staff. I put it here next to the tracking and control group so it has a friend."

The Chart

Take out your canvas and pencils, because it is time to draw up a nice organizational chart. You're probably familiar with these kinds of charts in your own organization, the ones with the bosses on top and you in some box way below them. It is a nice, clear way to describe some of the aspects of the project organization you are going to set up. It provides an overview of the chain of command, the authorization structure, and the tasks that a group of people are assigned to perform.

An organization is actually more than one person. If you are the project manager and you will handle all the tasks yourself, forget about this step and just go on and do your thing. However, in a normal project you cannot do everything by yourself; you are lacking the time, the knowledge, or the authority. If you look at how regular organizations are constructed, you'll realize that the principles are no different from project organization, except for the temporary nature of the project organization.

The executive (the boss) is the one with the knowledge about money, sales, and the market, and his employee knows how to build widgets. The one without the other is useless. Without the employee, there is nothing to sell, but without the executive there is no income to make the construction possible. You as a project manager will have to assemble a group of people that know how to do the programming, assess the business needs, test the applications, tie the infrastructures together, and so on. You construct a team that combines all the knowledge you need.

So draw it on the canvas: a box with only you in it and a larger box below it that contains all the people you need to do the actual job (the team).

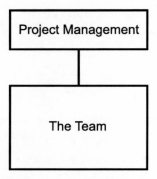

Figure 5-5: The Simplest Project Organization

If your team consists of only two people, I would almost say that you are done. If you have, say, twenty or more people on your canvas, there will be no way you can control that group, simply because you will have no time to do it and it will be just too much for one person to handle. Every person has a limit to how many people (and corresponding issues) he or she can take care of. Your *span of control* is limited. The easiest solution to this problem is to create groups.

You can segment the team by *specialization* (the specific knowledge they have; for example, programming, user insight, interfacing, data migration) or by a *part of the final product* that has to be constructed (for instance, the billing component or the collaboration of the business experts and programmers). In this way, each group has its own task, and by assigning a team leader that is responsible for taking care of a specific part of the project, you will only have to deal with the team leaders instead of the whole group.

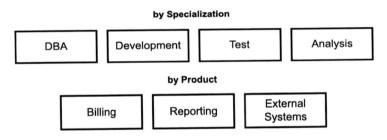

Figure 5-6: Segmentation by Specialization of Product

By segmenting your team, you introduce an extra layer of overhead. It will make your life a little easier but it will involve a certain cost, because of the need for extra time or people. When dealing with very large project teams, you can do this splitting up within a first level group, making it a real hierarchy. Just remember, you only do this to reduce the burden on the span of control of the person in charge.

Dividing the organization into groups also introduces the concept of responsibility. One person has the job of ensuring that a certain task will be performed. And when it comes to responsibility, there should be only one person held accountable. This avoids confusion, as it is always very clear whom to address about a certain topic.

An example of this technique is provided by the organizational structure in *Prince2*. In situations where multiple third-party vendors are involved, only one person is assigned the responsibility to take care of all aspects related to those vendors. Again, this prevents mix-ups and eases the burden of the project manager.

A project organization must survive within an existing corporate structure. This is a fact of project life. This means that you will have to deal with the structures of responsibility and authority that are already in place. The existing financial director may be the only one authorized to spend money. The corporation's sales director may be the only one authorized to make decisions about the sales process. And in a project, with all those changes that are bound to happen, decisions that have an impact on the standing organization must be made almost every day.

You need to incorporate the existing authorities into your project organization. In most methods, the project manager's authority is restricted by the project budget and limited to use of the assigned resources and leverage within the agreed-upon time scale. For example, if more money is needed, the project manager cannot simply spend it. He needs approval from someone authorized to give it.

To ease this process of obtaining authorization, an organizational entity above the level of the project manager is needed. One of the names you come across in this context is *steering committee*. This group is made up of managers from the existing organization who are authorized to make decisions about the project manager's operational constraints, such as ones involving money, time, quality, or the scale of the final solution.

As those managers are not always available, they frequently delegate that authority to one of their employees, who is then assigned to the project team. Because decisions often involve the business process as it relates to user interaction with the new system, this authority is usually passed on to a representative of the user organization, known as a *super user*.

Kick back, study your canvas, and draw that organizational chart!

Participation and Influence

We already discussed the need for some people to be involved in the project. However, there are multiple levels at which people can participate.

Try to avoid those people who offer little more than nuisance value, but if for some reason they must participate in the project, keep them as far as possible from any position of power.   For example, you can assign them to advisory boards that confer on project issues but have no real influence.

The insight you gained by performing a thorough stakeholder analysis will help you to determine the level of influence that best serves both the project and the individual.

You can then make more informed choices about exactly where in the organization each person should be assigned.

Relatedness (Interpersonal/Social)

- Covering Up Own Incompetence (Don't Rock the Boat)
  If you come across someone you suspect is covering up his or her incompetencies, steer clear!

- Boosting Another's Reputation (Sponsorship)
  Stakeholders that boost each other's reputation can work perfectly together side by side, but don't let them control each other.

- Undermining Another's Reputation
  Stakeholders that trash each other should not be in the same surroundings. It's preferable to avoid them altogether if you can.

- Attempt to Move to Another Job within the Organization
  Will not do much about his or her own job or assignment but can be found meddling in the desired area where he or she has no authority. Assign this person to the tasks under current authority. Perhaps he or she can serve in an advisory capacity for the area of the target function.

- Attempt to Build an Empire within the
  Organization
  Don't give such a person too much latitude.
  Everything will be artificially inflated.

- Attempt to Maintain an Empire within the
  Organization
  This person will block every change.

- Attempt to Gain More Latitude within
  Organization
  Makes assignments bigger than they actually
  are, so beware of inflation.

Of the People, by the People, for the People

Now you have in front of you a nice collection of boxes that
describe your project organization so far. In a project,
though, it's not boxes you must deal with but people
(remember, that is why you did the stakeholder analysis).

It's your job to fill in the boxes and take care of the
interests of the individuals you place inside them. You have
to align the following aspects:

- Skills

- Job description

- Position

- Workload

And you must align them in such a way that they are in harmony with the interests and goals of the project. You can do this by going back to the stakeholder interests checklist of Chapter 3.

Personal

- Work Orientation versus Family Orientation
  If someone has a strong family orientation, try to avoid assigning large workload requiring after-hours work or consider allowing to work remotely from home.

- Satisfaction with Current Job
  If not satisfied, consider including duties in the job description that provide greater satisfaction.

- Satisfaction with Current Organization
  You might consider some initial coaching or mediation before start-up.

- Desire to Gain More Skill/Knowledge in a Certain Area
  Include something that can improve person's skills and consider coaching or extra time for learning experiences (training, courses)

- Sufficient Appreciation
  Showing some appreciation can boost a person's performance.

- Reduction/Expansion of Workload
  Does someone want to do more or less? As a

project manager, you don't always have the authority to influence this, but you might give it a shot.

- Reduction/Expansion of Responsibility
  Actually, comments are the same as above.

- Infection by Not-Invented-Here Syndrome
  If infected, get person on board in some decision-making capacity. Assigning responsibility for certain aspects of the project might work wonders.

Relatedness (Interpersonal/Social)

- Recognition of Knowledge Among Peers Outside the Organization
  Put the person in a team among peers (for example, external consultant) and assign something of which he or she can be proud (such as writing an article or lecturing among peers about project features).

- Recognition of Job Competence within the Organization (Hierarchy)
  Make sure good work is noticed by assigning creation of progress reports about work or presentation of information sessions to stakeholders that should be informed about the matter.

Existence (Material Interests)

- Desire for More Money
  You might give it a shot, but most likely you have no real influence in this matter.

- Desire for More Tools
  Introducing some cool new tools might spark some motivation, especially among technical people.

- Desire for a Bigger Office
  You don't have to provide an entire kingdom, but when assigning locations, keep in mind that

Feedback

As a kid, I played this little game at school called *Telephone Line.* Twenty children huddled into a circle and one of us started by whispering a sentence into the ear of the neighboring kid, so that no one else could hear what was said. The message would be whispered from one child to the next in succession until it had come "'round circle." The fun of the game was in comparing what the last kid heard to what the first one originally said. Usually, the two sentences didn't even come close to sounding the same.

During a project, communication is the most effective tool a manager has for implementing a proposal, and this is especially true of feedback. This topic is so deserving of attention that almost the entire remainder of this book is devoted to it. There are three main reasons why feedback should be incorporated into the project:

1. To resolve an uncertainty (iterate to get the desired information; see "Project Strategy" section in the beginning of this chapter)

2. To reassure stakeholders that their interests are met (see Chapter 1)

3. To increase quality when a possible failure creates potential damage (using feedback to get more validation steps for a certain software component to increase its reliability and quality)

There are a lot of project management techniques and artifacts devoted to the subject of feedback, but it is not always clear in the methods they provide that it actually is a feedback mechanism you are getting. In the table below, I give some samples of artifacts that you can find in almost every method, along with explanations of the kind of feedback they provide.

I make an explicit distinction between feedback on the product and feedback on the process.

Product		
	Requirements Definition	Feedback to the users on how their requirements are noted after discussion, analysis, and negotiation
	Functional Design	Feedback to the users on how their requirements will be translated later on to a new system
	Prototype	Feedback to the users on how their requirements are translated to a new system
	Proof of Concept	Feedback to show if a certain concept is feasible
	Benchmark	Yardstick to provide later feedback on improvement or deterioration of a situation
	Test Results	Feedback on how design and requirements are implemented in a new system
Process		
	Schedule	Feedback on time constraints
	Budget	Feedback on cost constraints
	Progress Reports	Feedback on overall constraints, including quality and scope.

You might find this section to be rather short. Don't worry; all the other chapters will cover this subject.

CHAPTER SIX

Getting the Requirements for the Product

A friend of mine has a buddy who suffered through one of those can't-win situations with his girlfriend the other day. She accused him of not being romantic enough to arrange special occasions for the two of them to share. After responding with a spineless "Uhh . . .okay," this man took his lady to an absurdly expensive restaurant featuring soft music, fine wine, and elegant décor. She refused to enter the place, protesting that it was too extravagant and they couldn't afford it. All her stunned boyfriend could manage to choke out was, "WHAT?"

Figure 6-1: Miscommunication—We Talk a Lot but Have Different Things in Mind

Stop and think for a moment of all the times when you thought you understood what someone was saying, only to later discover that you were utterly wrong. Wilson, the neighbor of Tim Allen's character in the television program *Home Improvement,* would say, "The limitation concerns human bias in the selection and use of data. These biases arise because humans use less than optimal heuristics when retrieving and processing information." Basically, we are too narrow-minded and not open enough.

At this point in a project, we have to determine what the requirements are for the end result. We have to get it out of the heads of the stakeholders and onto a piece of paper. And that is one difficult job. Often, what is expressed in the sentence of the first stakeholder is very different from the software the last user will see. The most widely used and efficient way of getting the requirements is by asking. By talking to key stakeholders, like future users of the system, the needed information will emerge. It might seem obvious that this should be as accurate as possible; however, it is crucial to do it correctly at this stage. Although information systems are expensive to develop, changes made after a system has been completed are 50 to 100 times more expensive than making the same changes during the requirements determination activities.

And that's a hell of a job. I already mentioned the difficulties in understanding each other, but there is another catch. You have to anticipate the ways the tasks will change when they are running under the new system. Watts S. Humphrey would even go so far as to say:

> Requirements by their very nature cannot be firm because we cannot anticipate the ways the tasks will change when they are automated [. . .] Unless the job has previously been done and only modest changes are needed, it is best to assume that the requirements are wrong.[16]

When talking about requirements to the product, you think almost exclusively of the user community. However, don't forget about the other stakeholders that you analyzed: IT people, indirect users of the system (for example, the customers of the people using the product), and, as I explain at the end of this chapter, corporate policies.

In this section, the determination will be done by means of a workshop with the key stakeholders. A workshop is a kind of discussion between key stakeholders, with a moderator who manages the process. It is dynamic, and it should be fun. Whiteboards are used. Big screens and flashy presentations are featured. People should walk around a lot. And, of course, this show should produce a real end product: a set of requirements. It can be one workshop or many, depending on the scope of the project. This chapter deals with preparing and conducting a workshop and what to do with its results.

The activities in this section are not project management tasks. Of course the planning part is, but conducting the workshop isn't. However, because of the workshop's importance and the impact of requirements on the complete process of the project (remember, they're still a reflection of the stakes of the stakeholders), the software project manager should at least be aware of its pitfalls. If the project is large (read "small") enough, it is recommended that the project manager also conduct the workshop or at least be present for its discussions.

Approach

You already have a list of stakeholders, a goal and scope for the project, and some idea about the business priorities. Now you have to hammer out some requirements on paper. After conducting your risk assessment, you should have some indication about the risk that the requirements will not accurately reflect what the system should be in reality. I go with the comment of Watts Humphrey in the beginning of this chapter: the requirements will be wrong.

That is no problem. Just be aware of it and prepare for it. In this chapter, the goal is to get an initial, relatively workable set of requirements on paper to at least make a first step. In Chapter 8, I discuss how you can use the mechanism of feedback to zoom in on the right requirements.

You can use several iterations of a requirements determination process to improve the requirements. A lot of users are taking the IKIWISI approach to requirements for a system: I'll Know It When I See It. That is just swell, but you simply must make at least one round before you can iterate. You have to have a first set of requirements to jump-start the entire process.

Workshop: A Means for Getting the Requirements

Now you're ready to conduct a workshop to get a preliminary set of product requirements. What's the best way to set it up? You can think of the process as simply following a recipe for a successful workshop, one that calls for the ingredients and steps I provide in the remainder of this chapter. Cooking skill is not required, but you may need to customize the recipe to suit the occasion (project) and personal tastes (stakeholder interests). As with baking a cake, putting together a workshop starts with preparation.

Preparing the Workshop

The end result of the requirements determination activities should of course be a set of requirements. The representation of this set is treated later on in this chapter. A point to address at this moment is the depth of it all. How far should you go into detail? There is, as you might have expected, no concrete answer. The criteria you should use at all times are that the requirements be unambiguous and that all stakeholders have an identical view of what the requirements mean. You must use your own judgment on this one, but to be able to judge you must know the tasks that will be changed as part of the project.

And that's where it all starts, by *educating the project manager*. The project manager should monitor the stakeholders for a while as they perform their daily tasks. This is the only way to get a feeling for the subjects. However urgent everything might be, take the time to do this. It will pay off in the end. It helps you build a sense for the processes, for the business case, and for the entire organizational context. It is important to approach the issues from these angles, with the widest and most inclusive perspective.

Most users, as well as other stakeholders, tend to formulate their requirements based upon their current situations. They see where they are now and can only talk about the two or three steps they want to take from their current positions. This is a handicap because it limits the possibilities. Seen from a market, business, or process perspective, this practice falls short because it ignores opportunities that could be taken. Instead of talking about "extra data fields in our customer entry screen," stakeholders should address the things they want to do for a customer and then reason their way back from this to what information is needed to do it.

It sounds obvious, and it is. For an information analyst, this might be peanuts. But for most people, it tends to be very difficult. During the actual requirements determination, you need the stakeholders to be completely holistic (Ohmm, let your mind flow freely in the space that surrounds you). So, you have to *educate the stakeholders* before starting this phase. Let them attend a seminar on the future of the market, let them brainstorm about how their jobs are an integral part of the company's process, whatever. Let them view their tasks as part of the whole.

Checklist

In the preparation for the workshop, you can follow this checklist of aspects to consider:

- General Information (title, place, and time)
- Purpose
- Scope
- Subjects
- Controversy
- Strategy
- Result

133

- Participants

- Roles

- Tools

- Feedback/Follow-up

- Agenda

In the remainder of this section, these aspects will be treated in more detail. With these points in mind you can cover the basics for a successful workshop.

General Information

Starting off with some general information, your workshop's got to have a title, a name by which to call the beast. Make it short and clear, not worthy of a Victorian novel. "Workshop on Order Entry" is a good one. Pick a date and place. I will not say a thing about the place. Actually, a nice book that even includes maps on how your room should look is James Martin's *Rapid Application Development*.[17] It's a classic, so just read the original.

Concerning a time to set for the workshop, I just want to mention that the unit of duration for a workshop should be a part of the day (two parts make one day, so pick either morning or afternoon). Don't drag people out for only one hour. That's not a workshop; that's a conversation.

Purpose

What is the workshop all about? Purpose, scope, and subjects are what define the actual workshop. The purpose is important to inform the workshop participants correctly up front so that they have no wrong expectations, or at least to make the chances of that happening a little smaller. By the way, you don't have to yank all the information into one sentence; it's okay to make a paragraph out of it. "Partial requirements in the preliminary decision-making phase" is a sentence, but it tells virtually nothing. If the requirements coming out of the workshop are not final but will be reviewed and approved by some hot shots afterwards, write it like that! It won't win you the Nobel Prize for literature, but it sure will save your workshop.

Scope

The purpose places the workshop within the context of the project, and the scope tells us all about the actual content (for example, "order entry for 24-hour delivery"). The scope should also determine the field that will be covered, including a good definition of its boundaries. "How a new information system will have to support our order entry activities for 24-hour deliveries. Current activities may be subject to change." That second sentence is very important. If things may be altered, make that clear to keep people from having to read between the lines, but be careful about the words that you choose. The opposite holds true also, of course. If something is not allowed, state that: "How a new information system will have to support our order entry

135

activities for 24-hour deliveries. The new order entry activities as described in Large Document X and approved by Big Guy Y have to be considered."

Subjects

To create a good list of subjects to cover, some homework has to be done. A good preparation would be joining stakeholders in their work activities for a short time, as mentioned earlier in this section. In addition to this, you should talk to someone with knowledge about the scope. A good starting point, if possible, is to consider the tasks that fall into the scope, like these for order entry:

- Finding the customer

- Getting the order

- Checking for stock

- Placing the order

- Tracking the delivery

Another way is to make a distinction in categories of the subject at hand. If you order an ad in a newspaper, you have the little public announcements and the larger display ads to consider. When you're addressing a customer base, you can talk about large customers and small customers. There are green balls and yellow balls. Take your pick. There are a thousand ways to organize your subjects. They should be clear, logical, "feel good" distinctions that make immediate sense to the participants.

Controversy

Here's an open invitation to controversy: "How a new information system will have to support our order entry activities for 24-hour deliveries. The new order entry activities as described in Large Document X and approved by Big Guy Y have to be considered." State a purpose like that for your workshop and you know you will have some trouble. Most probably, someone in the workshop is no fan of Big Guy Y and thinks Big Guy Y doesn't know a thing about order-taking. However, the Large Document X is approved and is the basis for the workshop. Like I said, you've got T-R-O-U-B-L-E.

Perhaps one of the workshop's subjects is reorganized for the hundredth time. Maybe "ISO Certification" is the soup du jour (hype of the day) at the company, so everyone just wants to write large documents. Possibly the same workshop took place last year and no one heard a thing about that one. Controversy about the subjects of the workshop lies in wait. Find it. You really need help with this one. Again, talk to people and listen to them.

Strategy

Given the potential controversies and the list of subjects you put on the form in the previous steps, you should determine how to handle things, how to approach the subjects strategically. I know I said that the goal is to make everyone a winner. Take care of all stakes, but remember that most likely not everyone in the workshop is feeling lucky, thanks to the controversies. And if some people don't want to be

137

involved with the project in the first place, they can frustrate the process of conducting the workshop. If they are out to sabotage the whole works and are not into the win-win mood, you will not turn them from the Dark Side, at least not during the workshop. You can handle them later on. Be pragmatic about the situation. You also need an end result, so don't let them block your workshop.

For the Big Guy Y hater, accept it as a given. This is the way it is and you can't do a thing about it, so stop whining. Be passive or confrontational, whatever flavor you have up your sleeve (smell that shirt!). For this ISO thing, you might try making the issue bigger, bolder, and more abstract. For instance, if someone yaps about documenting every little thing, try using small steps to make the proposed procedure frighteningly larger: "Yeah, you are right. You should document whatever you do and have a great structure to support that. You want everything stored in one place so you can access it from anywhere. Of course, for that to be truly effective, you should also register this, and that, so you can cross-reference it with [ad nauseam]." If you can avoid the temptation to be sarcastic and can actually sound sincere, the person in question will respond that he or she is not ready for that yet. I really love this one. Try it.

The purpose of this step in the preparation of the workshop is to encourage you to think up front about the strategies you might have to use. In this way, you can prepare some information or invite someone on your side to the workshop to neutralize the controversy.

Result

What will you have when the workshop is over? The outcome will be the requirements of the end result of the project, and these can be written down as a story, documented as a formal specification in some cryptic scientific notation, or displayed with some cool graphics. There is so much research done on this subject, covering issues like how to check a set of inconsistencies or how to create a graph from here to eternity.

Just use whatever medium the key stakeholders are accustomed to using. If they like to tell stories, tell a story. If they are mathematicians, use formal calculus. If they are computer scientists, use bloody graphs. I like to tell stories myself. Envision beforehand what the result will look like and think about how you can read it. Close your eyes and see it!

And Finally, the Rest . . .

To finish your preparations, you can specify the participants of the workshop. Note who they are, what their positions are within the organization, and, most importantly, why they are invited to the workshop. In other words, note what role each participant plays in the discussions (leader, chairman, scribe, and so forth). If you want to use tools during the workshop, you should write them down and arrange for them to be there when needed.

This one deserves some emphasis: *In which way will the results of the workshop be communicated back to the participants, and what are the next steps for these results?*

It is only at this stage that you should create an agenda for the workshop, because it isn't until the end of these preparations that you have enough information to create a good agenda. That's enough of dipping your toes in the water at the edge of the lake. Now let's jump in and swim.

Conducting the Workshop

You are standing at the front of a room, and you are not alone. There are more people in the room, some that you know and some that you don't. They are all staring at you, and you have some idea about what they are thinking. Or at least you think you do, because you prepared this workshop as described. These people come here to defend their turf, to conquer new ones, to enhance their power, to reduce the influence of others, or, basically, just to kill time.

Thinking back about the flow of the stakes, you remember what you are supposed to do. You have to fulfill everyone's wishes today. The people in the room have their issues, their stakes, and each will proclaim his or her own stake as the topic of the day. If you are trying to defend your department's independence, you will not be happy with an information system that integrates all processes and makes your employees, or at least the things they do, obsolete. You want to have separate systems for all processes and hold on to your empire in between. You will probably try a different argument, using terms like *easier to maintain, better to control*, and *more transparent* to mask your true issue.

Formulating the Requirements

So there you are, sweating bullets at the front of the room. You, together with the members of the workshop, have to formulate the requirements for the end result of the project. It's a software project, so a system will be a large part of this end result. This set of requirements should address all the stakes of the stakeholders and, at the same time, pose no conflicts. If one requirement says the button should be blue and another says it should be green, then you will have requirements that you know will be impossible to fulfill.

This sounds difficult, and it actually is, but with enough time and patience you can go a long way towards solving this problem. Usually, though, time is not on your side, so you should try to get a reasonable set of requirements by the end of the workshop. Compromises, concessions, and a little force enter the mix of tactics that the project manager must use. Everybody should be a winner, and today!

Can you satisfy all the needs of everyone? Can you take care of all their stakes? Can you make everyone happy on this one day? Probably not everyone. As I mentioned before, people who are biased against the project before it even starts can disrupt the whole process of conducting the workshop. They may not yet have embraced the win-win frame of mind and may be intent on causing damage, and they can easily do so. You probably won't win them over today, but there's always tomorrow. You can deal with them later on, but right now you cannot afford to have them disturb the flow of the workshop. They should not have

141

been invited to attend, anyway. Sometimes, sadly, you have to include those you know are against you from the get-go, but you can block this opposition by having some colleagues who endorse your efforts sitting in on the workshop. Or you can invite a senior manager who will get detractors to just shut up.

Getting the Right Information

How can you get the right information out of the people that are in front of you (remember, you are hosting a workshop)? I thought about this complex question for a long time, and I came up with one answer: Ask.

If you know that you are not a talker or that you are an introvert who has limited communication skills, this workshop leader gig is not for you. If you have no problems communicating with others, then be yourself and just ask. Here are some strategies that work well for me:

- *Be stupid.* Don't be a smart-ass. Even if you already know all of it, let the participants be the stars. They are the experts.

- *Ask what you already know.* Start, for example, with a question about something you already know. Say something you know to be incorrect to get the participants' attention and see who corrects what. Most of the time, this gives you some glimpse of stakes.

- *Repeat.* If someone tells you somethihng, just repeat what was said using different words. In this way, you can get a consistency in words that are used.

- *Ask five times.* Ask for the "why" five times, and that will give you the highest level of reason. Ask for the "how" five times, and it will bring you to the lowest level of operation.

While the workshop leader is going through the process from left to right and top to bottom, the scribe should record all the statements made. Every record should include a label indicating who made the statement. When distributing the record of the statements and, later on, the requirements, the applicable name should always appear. This will keep people committed to what they said. If they just yell out something and their names are permanently associated with what they yelled, they will be more careful about what they say in the future.

At the end of each day, for example, or by the end of the workshop at the latest, the statements should be reviewed by the participants and approved. Group the statements together by subject and try to rephrase them with the participants' help so that they use the same language and try to avoid, or at least clarify, conflicting statements. The last action is to specify appropriate statements as requirements and to try to establish some priorities among them. A mechanism often used is to classify requirements as must-have, nice-to-have, and oh-well-this-is-just-a-suggestion.

This last point is a crucial one. You simply must prioritize your requirements because later on you will have to make plans and decisions about them, as everything probably can't be done, or at least can't be done at once. You have to get some indication about what is considered important and what is not.

Within the DSDM method (*www.dsdm.org*), the scheme used is called MoSCoW, which stands for:

- *Must Haves:* fundamental to the project's success

- *Should Haves:* important, but the project's success does not rely on these

- *Could Haves:* can easily be left out without impacting on the project

- *Won't Have This Time 'Round:* can be left out this time and done at a later date[18]

I stated in the beginning of this section that the purpose of the workshop is to establish requirements on the end result of the project (the product, which may also include organizational issues and procedures). However, sometimes statements are made on the way the project will be conducted (the process). Create a separate list for these statements and provide them to project management for consideration. Just make sure you tell the workshop participants that these process statements are treated differently.

Representing the Requirements

You have all your requirements in front of you on a piece of paper. You smell the paper. You feel the paper. You sense the emotions that are attached to the requirements. You close your eyes, and you have these images, these colorful blurs, and you are in touch with the minds of the stakeholders. You are the stakeholder profiler. You have to get the stakes out of the requirements.

Group all the requirements together per stakeholder. Try to formulate the stakes that are behind them. It's difficult, it's rather vague, and it's very "soft," but it's the information you are after. Remember, the requirements will likely change during the course of the project, but stakes remain the same. The requirements themselves will be represented in the way you defined them in the preparation of the workshop. All the participants will have their own versions and will be confronted by the stuff they wished for, as every requirement has the name of who said it attached to it.

This would be one way of doing it. There are a lot of techniques and formats available for use in writing your requirements. The right way depends on your approach. If you are going to have a lot of iterations and feedback, some *user stories* might be sufficient. This technique is used within Extreme Programming to get a first level of statements about the system. They are best viewed as some one-liners about what the system has to do. The purpose of these stories is to be able to plan the next iterations and get some estimates. In his article, "Structuring Use Cases with

Goals," Alistair Cockburn points out that these in fact are not real requirements but just *stories*.

The fewer iterations and feedback rounds you are planning to have, the more you should structure and formalize the registration of the requirements. In the same article, Cockburn analyzes the different uses of *use cases*. There are different use cases out there, but in essence they reflect "the ways in which a user uses a system."[19]

The different versions that Cockburn found have different aspects:

- *Purpose*: Are they real requirements or are they stories?

- *Contents*: Is the notation formal or informal, is the content contradictory or is it harmonized?

- *Structure*: Does the technique require a formal prescribed structure or can you write it in an almost free format?[19]

The more harmonized and formal descriptions are easier to develop, simply because computers are formal and cannot handle contradiction, something that also holds true for most developers.

However, harmonization can take you a lot of time to reach, and analyzing and negotiating can also consume much precious time. Also, a formal notation and structure can slow you down in writing out requirements. And finally, formal notations don't go well with "normal" people (non-techies). If they are your primary audience, you should tone down the formality.

For project management and perhaps some key stakeholders, it may be wise to have some representation of the stakes, which may help to refine the definition of the stakes. Taking a cue from professional FBI profilers, you could use some great slides along with a photo of each stakeholder and a list of the crimes (stakes) he or she committed.

Figure 6-2: Profiling Your Stakeholders

Policies are Requirements Too

Why did the chicken cross the road? To get to the other side. Now for something a little more difficult: Why do the English drive on the left side of the road? Personally, I have no idea where this left-side business comes from and, personally, I don't care. These islanders apparently made an agreement at one point and stuck to it, just to avoid running into each other. Why does the software I want to buy for the company have to comply with J2EE standards, ISO

standards, or any other specified standards? First of all, I don't
know what they mean, and secondly, why should I care? If you
eat out, you don't care if they use a Siemens or a Philips
microwave to nuke the food. However, you do want to keep
your stomach at ease.

At companies large and small, there will be some
statements made about what your software should look like
and to which specifications it must comply. Here's the
skinny on the policies: they're annoying, they're anonymous,
and they're here to stay. "All information systems should
have a 3-tier architecture": this is what a typical policy looks
like. In case you stumble across one, you will recognize the
beast. It actually sounds like a requirement, doesn't it? And
no wonder; it actually is.

Policies can be viewed as requirements made by the
company itself. Following the philosophy of this book, the
company should have stakes. I know that I argued earlier
that only individuals have stakes, as it is a person who has
fears and wishes. At the end of it all, I'm not taking that
back. Only with company stakes, it's difficult to pinpoint
their original owners. These can be the board of directors,
your boss, or the policy department (those guys walking
around in togas and proclaiming the patently obvious as
Nobel Prize-winning stuff). They may also be stakes that are
inherent to operating a company, like "making a profit" so
"we should earn more than we spend."

Back to the original question: why does the software
I want to buy (or perhaps make) have to comply with certain
policies? For the same reason it has to satisfy the stakes of

148

the stakeholders; in other words, to make everyone a winner (including the company) so you have a happy and successful project. If the policies are the requirements, what are the stakes, and can you change the policies? Now, that's worth some thinking about.

Consider the situation in which a toga from the policy department descends from his ivory tower to the slimy mud of the software project. He has with him a parchment scroll whose contents he shares with you in a loud voice. "Hear, fools, hear. Thou shalt comply with these standards: J2EE, ISO, and OSI. Thou shalt use these techniques: UML, DPL, and JBF." The crowd goes wild, sets fire to his parchment scroll, and kicks him back up into the tower. However, his ivory tower is next to the palace of Zeus, the Almighty Boss, who hears the whining of the toga and sends his thunder upon your little project. "THOU SHALT COMPLY."

You can ignore the policies, but you will get trampled upon if you do. You can fully comply with them, but then you will have stuff that no one wants, at least no one with money to pay for it. So you have to dive into the stakes that are behind the policies. Luckily, most of the time they are good ones, things that really benefit your project, your company, and, in the end, you.

Thou Shalt Use the Big O

What are the stakes? I cannot be specific, as they can be a lot of things, but perhaps some examples I encountered may help you on your way. "Every database should be Oracle" (or just pick a vendor you like). When buying a system, it can be simple. "Does it run Oracle? No? Sorry, we don't want it." Normally, however, you buy functionality and not technology. You buy a system for what it can do and not because the bits and bytes are flipped in a certain way. For normal use, you buy a car to get you from point A to point B and not because it has yellow spark plugs. You can ask the supplier to port its system to the desired database vendor, but then you get a special version of the system (which is a nightmare in maintenance), and it's likely that the supplier has limited knowledge about this particular database.

The stake here has to do with sharing database administrators among several systems. The company benefits from efficient use of employees, especially when it comes to specialized people. Database administrators (DBA's) are a good example. Having more similar systems that these people can maintain will make the costs of maintenance drop. Using a more mainstream database like Oracle also makes it easier to get some outside people from the market to do the tasks when your own employees are overloaded or not available.

In this case, it is not that the database should be Oracle but that we should make efficient use of the current DBA's and should also have no problem finding outside people to handle the system. Now, that's a company stake!

What Language?

Someone told me once, "If it ain't programmed in Java
following the Extreme Programming principles, we don't want
to buy the software." Arguing about why he put this
statement so firmly, the person orated for an hour on the great
advantages Java has in respect to more traditional programming
languages. And in combination with principles from Extreme
Programming, the resulting software would be perfect. He was
talking about policies put into a system he was going to buy.

Do you really care in what language your word
processor is written? Delphi, Smalltalk, C++, or Miranda?
You probably don't. Then why should you care when it's a
specific information system you buy? You should pay
attention to this aspect, that's for sure, but not because the
syntax is so neat, and certainly not because some external
bureau (or a guru at a seminar) has hollered that Java is the
way to go.

So why should you consider these aspects? For the
use of the software itself, you don't care what is under the hood;
if it runs, it runs. But for the continuation of the system down
the road, it is a factor to consider. If an obscure programming
language is used, it may be difficult in the future to find good
programmers skilled in this particular language. This is
definitely a risk for the quality of the software in the long run;
as you know, people come and people go, including
programmers. As for programming principles, let everyone
program in the way that works for them best. Just look for
principles; are they available and used? The company's only

stake is to have no surprises in either the quality of the software or the process of constructing the software.

As before with the stakes, you can do something with these language requirements. They're valid business arguments and they leave some room for maneuvering. Are you still wondering what the stakes were for the guy that told me "If it ain't programmed in Java . . ."? I guess he had programmers in his organization who wanted to program using way cool techniques they had learned at a seminar. But that's just my guess.

Are You Thin?

Software architectural discussions are always the best. You draw four boxes with several arrows between them and state that all systems should comply with this architectural design. "All systems should use a 3-tier architecture." I will not explain what it is (if you want to know, just look it up), except to say that in the segment where I operate there are very few systems that follow this architecture (at the moment when I'm writing this book). So, do you have to build it yourself?

Searching for the stakes in this case took me quite some time. It involved talking to togas, dissecting their arguments, turning them over, looking at them from up close, looking at them from far away with my eyes almost shut, and so on. The effect of this policy is that in workstations there is less software installed than for traditional, so-called thin-clients, which seems to result in a system that is easier to maintain. The second consequence seems to be less network traffic, requiring less bandwidth to be purchased and therefore saving the company some money.

In the end, ease of maintenance and saving money on bandwidth are the original stakes of the company. Die-hard technicians might now complain, "That's not the real power of 3-tier." Perhaps they're right. The point is that it doesn't matter. The requirement is formulated, correct or incorrect, but it's the stake that's important. So before redesigning your system, you can consider cheaper alternatives for saving money on bandwidth and increasing ease of maintenance. You go against the policies, but you do it by presenting the substitute requirements in such a fashion that they keep supporting the stakes. Most of the time, this approach is a winner. It is at least worth a discussion.

CHAPTER SEVEN

Getting the Requirements for the Process

After reading the chapters so far, you'd love to go spiral or incremental and hog wild on the feedback loops, all the while taking your time to do things well and do them in the way you want. This chapter is here to spoil that illusion. Either management or your customer, or both, will put some restrictions on the process because they have requirements to that process.

The most obvious are time and cost restrictions. You may not run the project forever and you may not create your own corporate money pit. You will have to take care of the

155

constraints put on the project. Furthermore, the strategies I discussed earlier in this book are not all very well known to the general public. The traditional plan-driven approaches are beloved by managers in general. They produce an aura of predictability and control. As discussed earlier, this is not always the case, but people don't like handing over a blank check while having no clue as to what they will get in return.

Managing Constraints

We Dutch are cheap, or at least that is what's suggested. In Belgium, it is claimed that the Dutch are buried face downwards to create more slots in which to park our bicycles. I think you can say that we try to avoid spending too much money. If you managed a software project here in the Netherlands, you would see a very strong tendency to save as much money as possible. However, I've never heard of a place where there is an unlimited budget.

My cheapness (from being Dutch) is an illustration for the more earthier matters concerning a project: trying to get a fix on the limited mundane stuff you need to proceed to the more noble cause of building a system. Whatever you have to create, whatever the reason for the project may be, there will always be *constraints* set for the project. These conditions determine the space in which the project organization may operate. Therefore, you might think of this part of project management as the "party pooper" segment, as constraints always spoil the fun.

Project constraints consist of the following elements:

- *Cost*: This includes everything that costs money, like people and equipment.

- *Time*: What is the time frame in which every activity should take place?

- *Quality*: What is the level of quality the project has to reach?

Constraints are not independent from each other. Reaching a higher level of quality will cost you more money. If you want to use less time, you need more people (later on in this chapter, you will see that adding more women to give birth to one child does not shorten the nine-month gestation period; this is rocket science project management). The point I'm trying to make is that constraints *are interdependent*.

A classic way to show this interdependence is through use of the Project Constraints Triangle, or Iron Triangle. Imagine a 3-D space where the x-axis represents the amount of cost, the y-axis the amount of time, and the z-axis the level of quality for the project.

The project is represented by a triangle within this 3-D space. The size of a project is displayed as the square of the triangle. The size is determined by complexity and the amount of the product to realize. As you might understand, quality is a product requirement, and size can be viewed as the *scope* of the project.

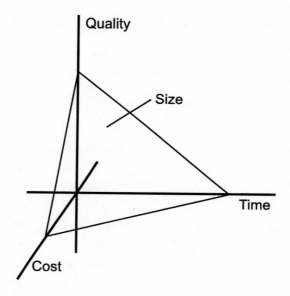

Figure 7-1: Iron Triangle of Project Management

A project with a constant size can have altering constraints. However, altering one constraint has influence on the others because the square of the triangle stays the same. The constraints are reflections of the stakes of the customer, but keep in mind that regardless of how boldly the constraints are stated by the customer, they are requirements, not stakes, so there is room for some negotiation. Playing with the aspects of the project triangle (including size) may also satisfy the stakes of the customer and therefore are more likely to be accepted.

It seems that every customer wants the best product tomorrow, and it may not cost a penny. I'm sure these customers do exist, but most top managers have a more realistic view of the matter. They know constraints must leave some room to operate. This doesn't mean they will ever admit that.

Determining Constraints: Cost

Money is the universal language. Or is it sex? I always mix 'em up. Sex on a project can get you into jail, so I'll stick for the moment with money. Everybody can relate to an amount of dollars. Function points, lines of code (LOC), or mean error deviations on mantissa buffer overflows (MEDOMBO, yep, made this one up) may mean nothing to people, but money talks!

This is probably why stakeholders around a project put such a big emphasis on this subject. It is finally a language they can understand. The great thing is that most items can be expressed in terms of money. So money is truly the universal language.

During the actual running of the project, the project manager should watch that no more money is spent than is allocated for the project, and it would be good to create nice graphs to illustrate what the project's balance sheet looks like. Duh! Perhaps we will spend some time on this subject later, perhaps not.

At this moment, when the project is not actually started yet, or hardly is, we can consider the schizophrenic situation where money talks heavily but the thing to construct is not specified (this will be done during requirements determination). This is most like a conversation between a dad and his son when the son is going to buy a car . . .

> Son: "It must cost at least $ 50,000."
>
> Father: "You must have a car in the range of $25-30,000."

Neither of them said anything about a little red Corvette or a little purple Pinto. But they expressed their stakes directly into a metric, which they can compare. Dad was ripped off before by his daughter when she bought her car and he promised his wife that he wouldn't make the same mistake again, but he wants to pay some of the cost. Son just wants to cruise for babes and simply assumes that Daddy is picking up the tab. So if you were a negotiator on this one, forget the absolute amounts and focus on learning from the stakes.

If, for example, a system has to be built for a customer and the specification for it is 4 lines, and the customer wants it for not more then $10,000, the origin of this 10,000 figure would be the most valuable information a software project manager could get from this statement. The basis for specifying this amount might be:

- The previous project that the financial controller handled was originally estimated for $10,000 and went way over budget

- There is a procedure that allows a certain level of management to make investments up to $9,999, and to invest higher amounts one has to be a level up in the hierarchy

- Five years ago, the company asked for a quote on a completely different kind of system, which was $20,000, and the brother of the nephew of the vice president said that this current system was half the complexity of the former one

By knowing the reasons behind the requirements, you can deal with the amount. In the case of the first reason shown above, you can talk about a good way of tracing and tracking the budget with the controller to avoid an unexpected overrun. Be creative.

A great source of information is the way that a deal is either constructed or desired to be constructed by the customer (who can also be an internal customer): *fixed price* or *time-and-material* (T&M) based. In the first case, an exact amount is determined to deliver a certain product or service. In the second, the cost depends on the time and material actually spent and will therefore be calculated after the job is done.

With a fixed price basis, you really have to be sure you know exactly what you want in a product or service. Otherwise, you know in advance exactly what you have to pay for a system you may not need. With a time-and-material basis, you must be able to manage the project in such a way that it really ends and doesn't drag on for years and years. If you view statements about the construction of the cost in this light, you get more and more insight into the truth (it really is out there, you know).

To summarize, in relation to the money aspect you have to answer the following questions:

- What financial statements are already made in respect to the project?

- Who made these statements?

- Why did they make these statements (stakes)?

- Are there already statements on cost structure (fixed price versus T&M)?

- If yes, why are these statements (stakes) made?

- How can you satisfy these stakes in such a way that there will be some room created to change absolute amounts?

Note on the last question: Creating some room does not mean that you are actually going to change the amounts. The goal is to provide yourself with enough room to operate.

Determining Constraints: Time

"The bearing of a child takes nine months, no matter how many women are assigned."[3]

This is one of the most insightful observations on project management made within the last thirty-five years. It dates back to 1975 and was written by Frederick P. Brooks Jr. in *The Mythical Man-Month*. Welcome to the age of rocket science.

In the communication of the timing aspects of a software project, many mistakes are caused by the use of the man-month unit. As the words suggest, it indicates "a month spent by one person." For determining the cost of the project, it is a fairly good unit (for instance, "Building the darn thing takes 3 man-months"). You know what a guy costs per month, so you can do the math. But as time passes, this statement will be shortened to "3 months," either in actual written words or in the minds of the people involved.

"How long does the project take?"

"Oh, 3 months."

And then the fun starts.

"We need to finish the project sooner."

"We'll add a resource. Problem fixed."

The problem with this kind of reasoning is that some tasks cannot be split, due to sequential dependence or just because it is not possible (like the childbirth thing). The trick is that a man-month is an indicator for cost and not for *progress*. So, while considering and discussing time, be aware of this communication trap.

This may be the most valuable lesson, but it is not the only thing to consider about time at this moment. At this stage, a detailed planning will not be created (luckily), but a global time frame, with start and end dates, will surely be available, at least in the minds of the stakeholders concerned. Here holds the same thing as discussed in the paragraph on money: try to get a fix on why these dates are chosen. I give below only some of the possible reasons.

It should be finished by then because . . .

- the most important manager takes a holiday (paid in advance) afterwards

- another project will start directly after it, and people are already allocated for this

- someone just yelled out this date one day, and everybody has used the same mantra ever since

See if the stated deadline holds with the cause and target for this project.

You may perhaps miss something about planning and estimating stuff, but this will be treated after the requirements are known (Chapter 9). However, at this point some statements will be made about time, money, and effort. If you have to rely on the input of experts for this (programmers, analysts), the best and only thing you can do is to talk to them and get an estimate.

While doing this, focus on *why* they decided on this particular amount. If it is similar to what they have done in the past, change some of the details you tell them to see how that changes their behavior. Most of all, listen seriously to them and let it be *their* estimation. Otherwise, if you have to work with the people later on in the project, and you provided the estimate, they normally will not agree and will not feel committed to doing the work in your estimated time rather than theirs.

Even If You Don't Know, You Have to Say Something

"Son, what do you want to be when you grow up?"

"Well, Dad, I have no idea. Because I'm just 8 years old, I haven't evaluated my options yet. Hormonal changes will probably alter my preferences and with the pace of development in technology, it's hard to say what kind of new jobs will emerge in the future anyway."

If your kid creates sentences like these, be afraid . . . be very afraid.

A so-called "normal" child would just say, "Fireman, Dad." Then Dad would smile, open a trust fund to put his son through college in the future, and slap his kid on the back when he finishes his first year of medical school on his twentieth birthday. That's a familiar scenario!

Now Dad talks to his boss . . .

"Well, Project Manager (a.k.a. Dad), when will it be ready, and what will it cost?"

"Boss, I have no idea. The 'it' you are referring to is undefined, and the requirements are changing. The responsibilities are unclear and new people are assigned to the project from the user groups every day. It's best I take it one day at a time and we go incremental. I can tell you what the first increment will cost and when it will be ready, but don't ask me how many increments it will take . . . if we ever finish at all."

That should be familiar also. Dad is a professional software project manager. He knows Planning (capital intended) and has learned by experience that if he can't keep the promise, he should not make it. It's funny, though, that the two familiar scenes involve the same man. Why is it funny? Even though he knows that the chances of his son's becoming an actual fireman are slim, Dad is satisfied with the answer and saves money based upon whatever assumptions he has. He has no idea if his son will go to college or, if so, when, and he has no clue what it will actually cost at that time. Yet he still reserves money for the future of his son.

What might be Dad's problem with "it," which happens to be an information system? The answer provided to his boss is sincere and probably represents the truth. However, his boss can't wait around for such an answer; he must have some statements to be able to run his business. So even though his statements are true (let's assume), is it fair for Dad to claim that he has no idea?

Fair to whom? To himself? Well, he made his point and he told the exact view he has in his mind. But is it fair to consider only his own well-being? Should he provide some statements to his boss although he is highly unsure? Actually, the overall well-being of the company is also in Dad's own interest; if it goes bankrupt, he has no job (and his son will have no college fund). To keep the business healthy, the boss has to have some vision of the future. How long will my people be involved in this project (and therefore away from their day-to-day operations)? How much money do I have to reserve for this endeavor (you know, income and expenses should be in line with each other to run a business)? So in his own interests, Dad should provide some statements, just like his son.

Consider why his boss needs the claims for the future. First of all, he has to anticipate expenses and extra resources, but he also has to determine the overall course. All related activities within the company should be in tune with the strategy of this project. It's like crossing the ocean: you don't have to know the exact path you will sail, but just knowing that you aim to hit the coast at the opposite side will help you plan a welcome committee reception at the other end. Some kind of vision will help the boss steer the *complete* business in a specific direction, which will benefit Dad, his project, and the stability of his job, and so, in the end, will help him in raising his son.

Convincing Management about Your Approach

You have done your utmost best to assess risks and stakeholders, and you have created one beautiful approach that tackles all potential problems. You iterate several times, you spend a lot of feedback on verification, and you have some extreme new techniques thrown into the mix. Project Potion, remember?

As I mentioned in the introduction to this chapter, management likes to have predictability. One direct process to the end result looks like something that is easy to calculate and at least easy to understand. Go cyclic and you lose a lot of people, as they will not get it. So the correct way would be as described in the previous section. However, how can you get approval?

Actually, the best remedy would be to sum up the arguments outlined in this book and explain why you created the approach as it is. But you also have to provide some view of the overall project. Plan and estimate stuff you have absolutely no idea about; just make an informed guess and attach a huge disclaimer. They will need this for the big picture, the larger planning of the company.

The whole process of determining the approach is so important for the customer/management that I advise that you involve them in its construction. First, get your business priorities straight. Is the real issue marketing time, quality, or keeping the product cheap? Draw the Iron Triangle and explain to the stakeholders that they will have to make choices!

Software project management is a game of making choices and trade-offs. A lot of the necessary decisions are probably out of your reach because you are not authorized to make them. Get down with the people who do have this authority and tell them the story. If you find a risk on the requirements, an uncertainty about what should actually be built, by using Project Potion you can add multiple iterations into your strategy to make the requirements clearer in every step. You can also add some other feedback loops (discussed in Chapter 8). In both cases, you will have an increase in either cost or time, or both. Iterations take time and therefore involve higher costs. Feedback in general costs time to create, so here the same increase in cost holds true. But by using these two mechanisms, you increase the quality of the project end result.

Figure 7-2: Using Iterations and Feedback to Resolve Risks on Requirements Increases Cost, Time, and Quality

If you take a more generic view of this sample and make a translation to the concepts discussed earlier in this book, you get the following sequence:

1. Business priorities, risks, and interests of stakeholders determine the approach to be taken

2. Choices made in the approach (the actions you take) have an impact on the aspects of the Iron Triangle: cost, time, quality, and size

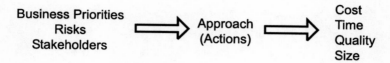

Figure 7-3: Priorities, Risks, and Stakes Determine the Project Approach; Which Approach Is Taken Influences Cost, Time, Quality, and Size

CHAPTER EIGHT

Feedback on the Product

How many times while dining out have you ordered a meal that was described on the menu as delicious, only to find out when it arrived that the cook went completely experimental on it? I read this incredibly appetizing description for a main course involving the better parts of a lamb. When the dish arrived, I noticed that it wasn't actually cooked. I like my meat extremely well done, nuked to the bone. Then I remembered that a menu is not a meal.

How many times have you brought your car to the garage for a routine check-up, only to hear later on from the mechanic that he took special care of the odd noise he heard?

171

Either you are going deaf or this guy is hearing sounds that are not there, but in any case you have to pay for this extra "service."

How many times have parents brought home a dog because "I wanna doggie" is screamed by some seven-year-old who later realizes that he didn't want the doggie itself but only the soft feeling of fur? The howling youngster would have been just as happy with a plush stuffed animal, and no one ever has to feed a teddy bear. You may think you want something, only to find out later you had no idea what you were actually wishing for. Having kids itself falls into this category.

♫ *How many times must a man...* ♫

Meanwhile, Back in the Jungle . . .

In the jungle of software project management, the fierce full application developer is searching for requirements. After a good hunt, he is dragging a bag full of statements back to his cave. There he grunts away for weeks on end, picking up each requirement, looking at it, smelling it, and taking it apart. Finally, the creature sets foot outside his cave for the first time in months. The daylight is hitting him hard. With him he drags a large ball made out of pieces of requirements. This exquisite creation is the result of his loving craftsmanship. He shows it to the rest of the tribe, holding it up, shining there in the sun. The tribal leader looks at it, smells it, and then sets fire to it. Anthropologists are still trying to figure out whether the leader was communicating his disapproval or merely providing warmth for the tribe.

172

Expectations

The central issue here is expectations. You imagine a certain situation in the near future. You close your eyes and you can actually experience it. You open them again and try to describe what you saw to someone else. This person will hear the same words and the same sentences that you are using, and the two of you might even share the same enthusiasm for it. But if you both think about "a nice woman" or "a nice man," the fact that you share the same warm feeling about the image that the words produce doesn't guarantee that the hair color of the imaginary friend is identical. It probably isn't. Communication is always influenced by the interpretation of a person.

Requirements in a software project are no different in this respect. An "easy to use interface" can be interpreted in hundreds of ways. So, is there nothing you can do? Wrong. You can do a lot, but it will take some effort. You can provide feedback by using a mechanism that is not affected by interpretation, or at least is less affected. Exchanging pictures of your idea about "a nice (wo)man" can solve the hair color issue. There are several available methods you can use for the product requirements of a software project. And that's what this chapter is all about.

Right Idea, Wrong Idea

It's not only the interactions with people that can cause problems. It's also your own imagination that plays tricks on you. What may seem nice in your head may be a disaster in reality, even if the other person understood you correctly. Feedback is the magic word here as well. It can help indicate that you or any others were wrong in some idea of the future at a relatively early time in the project.

Requirements validation is all about feedback. Is the interpretation of the requirements for the real-life situation correct, and are the requirements still valid? It's now feedback time!

Ways to Provide Feedback

Every issue concerning feedback starts out with three W-questions and one H-question:

- *What?* What is the subject of the feedback?

- *Who?* Who provides the feedback and who is the target audience?

- *Why?* Why do you provide the feedback? What is its purpose?

- *How?* What is the medium by which the information is transferred?

The "what" and "who" are treated in the remainder of this chapter, as some samples and suggestions are provided. That leaves us at this moment with the "why" and "how."

Why?

In my personal opinion, this is the most important question when determining a feedback mechanism: why are you doing it in the first place? Three reasons can be found to provide product feedback:

1. *Validation*

    It's a way to validate information/state of a current version of a product. With uncertain requirements, feedback tries to zoom in on the gaps and inconsistencies. As a famous sentence in our industry goes, "Did we build the right thing, and did we build it right?"

2. *Reassure Stakeholders*

    What more can I say? A large part of the first chapter goes on and on about the importance of reassuring your stakeholders about what is happening with their stakes/requirements. So even if *you* don't think you need to validate, showing the stakeholders that you are right is a smart thing to do.

3. *Risk of Miscommunication*

    When there is a large risk of miscommunication, it is advisable to provide some kind of feedback mechanism. For this situation, think about several parties that are not collocated and working on interdependent system components.

How?

If you take a very broad generalization, there are three types of media that can be used to provide information for feedback:

- *Verbal*: Nice expensive word for talking about the subject

- *Written*: Paper is patient, they say, but Word documents that are never printed can be considered within this category as well.

- *Mock-Up*: I am struggling for a nice word for this media form, but prototypes, screen prints in Powerpoint, and other means for creating a visual image of a future system can be considered as *mock-ups* (or "Hollywood" versions, as I will explain later in this chapter).

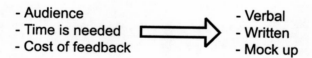

Figure 8-1: Aspects to Consider When Choosing the Means for Feedback

Every type has its own advantages and drawbacks. Verbal is fast and easy to do, but if you need to fall back on the issue a couple of weeks later, you can only hope that everybody remembers it correctly. Writing will overcome this last problem, but writing one large document with no images will virtually guarantee that not every user will be able to plow through all those words. Here's where some visual representation might help out, like a small prototype that shows users what the general idea of the new system is. But creating a mock-up costs time, and after you have used it, you will throw it away, so you must consider if it is worth the money.

That last paragraph actually outlined the aspects that you should consider in choosing the right medium for feedback on the product:

- *Audience*: Which medium is most likely to have the best reception?

- *Time at Which It Is Needed*: This refers to the time frame in which the information in the feedback is needed. If you need a decision on whether a green button is better than a blue one, once you have used a feedback mechanism, you probably won't need it again. If the information serves a formal (contractual) purpose, you need it available for future reference. If you have an outcome of a specification of an interface, you need the field definitions available for future use.

- *Cost of Feedback*: Every medium has its own cost. Consider if the use of the medium is worth the cost.

Overview

If I put all the previous information in one overview, we get the following:

- Risk and stakeholder analysis provide you with potential issues. Some of these issues can be resolved by using a feedback mechanism on the product.

- *Why* you are going to use feedback is the most important question. Is the problem you want to address an issue of validation, reassuring stakeholders, or cutting miscommunication risks? *Who* and *what* flow automatically from the risk and stakeholder analysis.

- If you know why you want to use feedback, you can address the question of *how* you are going to do that. An important aspect of this is the cost of the measurement. It may cost more money, take more time, or influence the quality of the end result. This is the link with the process part of project management. The cost may be unacceptable; in other words, the way in which you want to resolve a certain risk gets too expensive. In that case, the buck stops here.

- If costs are acceptable, you have yourself a nice feedback mechanism.

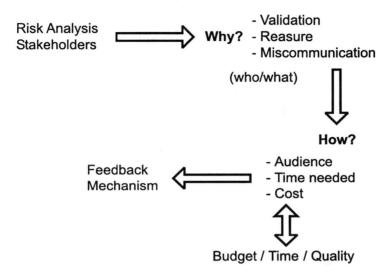

Figure 8-2: Integrated View of Product Feedback Considerations

Global to Detailed

In my hometown, a complete new neighborhood was built, with houses, roads, parking spaces, and everything else brand new. Even the people were new. I don't know how it is in the rest of the world, but in Holland such a new area has to have a new work of art. And for $300,000, the locals have their say in choosing what kind of concrete artwork with holes and circles they want to have (yep, it's called "participation").

The first requirement is set by City Hall: The art piece should reflect the struggle between man and the water (we live on the coast, you know, but "the struggle between man and the government" would be more appropriate).

179

Next, ten artists are asked to put in their suggestions. Vague drawings of holes and squares, circles and sockets, black and blue blobs are offered. The intention is that the inhabitants get an idea of what they can have in front of their doors. Everybody can vote (I make no funny remarks about the U.S.'s 2000 election, and that's difficult). The three winners go to the next round. They make a detailed work drawing of the actual construction of their art piece. Is it steel? Is it placed in water? Is it green? Is it ugly? Based upon the final drawings, the government chooses. Steel? Water? Green? Ugly? Yep, yep, yep, and yep again.

Software Design

You know, creating a piece of software is also a work of art. Luckily, there is no voting with the residents; otherwise, no system would ever be built. But the mechanism of taking a requirement and creating first a global drawing and afterwards a more detailed sketch is similar. We wouldn't be fair to the profession if we hadn't a great name for it: a *design*.

If we have good requirements, they will not say too much on how a system should be built. It should provide us with statements on what it should do and in what context, and perhaps, sometimes, on how it should be performed. All technicians that read the previous chapter would have wondered, "Where is my design?" Well, here you are. Designs are in fact a way of communicating how a software system should be constructed.

They are a description of what will be the end result. In this respect, it's one of the earliest points in time when stakeholders can see some glimpses of what is done with their requirements. So, when all the techies go to work, the project manager should make sure they maintain consistency between the design choices and the original requirements.

Global versus Detailed

What is global and how deep is detailed? There you've got me. Draw a line somewhere where it feels natural. If you look at a system as boxes, the global design places the boxes within a certain context along with their dependencies. The detailed design fills in the boxes. Another way of looking at it is by considering the functional versus technical aspects. The first design (or specification, for now the differences are too tiny to discuss) masters the points on how to handle the system from a user perspective. What should the user do and what will the system do? The second phase covers the technical implementation of the functional one. What data to manipulate? Which file to copy where? This approach reflects the opinion that techies can never lead the design process and the functional aspects rule!

In either way, you start your translation of the requirements to the real world by making designs or specifications. It is of course a communication tool for the technicians within their own species, but stakeholders want to see what happened with the things they yelled, and this is their first opportunity, so you'd better take care.

Designs and Normal People

After reading the previous section, I know you get my point. However, I will spend some more text on the matter, because it's too important to shortchange, and the natural tendency within software projects is to consider designs as a product of their own. "We design to create a design." Wrong, wrong, wrong. A design is a medium to explain how the requirements will be translated to the real world. And there lies the problem for project management with specifications and designs; the designs are considered to be a word passed from one technician to another. The global expert tells the detailed expert, who tells the developer what to do, and they all pass their messages by the medium called design. They leave out the non-technicians, the "normal" people.

During the actual construction of the specifications, the software project manager will not be involved too much in the discussions, and if he is, it's not because he has the role of project manager. The biggest challenge for the manager is to make sure the communication to the stakeholders is done effectively and in a timely manner. He should make sure that once in a while the software gurus come out of their caves and describe in understandable words what they are envisioning. These discussions are legendary: two vastly different worlds colliding with each other. Try to order something in Paris and you catch the drift.

Enhancing the Chances of Success

The project manager can do something to enhance the chances
for the success of this process. First, you must be aware of it,
and you now are. Second, the choice of the guy or gal leading
the design activities should not be based solely upon technical
know-how; communicative skills should have even more
weight. And, last in the "open door'" series, take more time for
the specifications than you think you need. Take the time to
create designs. You will earn it back later on. However, use the
extra time for communicating with the stakeholders, not for
making your graphics look even slicker.

The communication between the designers and the
stakeholders can take place in workshops and other kinds of
meetings. So the project manager—that means you—can
check if such meetings are planned and held or can even
actively schedule such sessions or emphasize the need for
them. After such a meeting is held, schedule a talk with one
of the stakeholders to see if the necessary information was
communicated.

Documenting It All

To ensure that the information is presented in such a way that
the stakeholders can understand the specifications, the
designers should keep track of all the decisions they made
and, more importantly, the arguments for why they made a
certain decision. If they decide to use Super XML Parser
sub-system GNA (don't try to find this one), somewhere
there should be a record of the fact that they intend to use it

and the arguments on why they chose this sub-system and not another one. If they talk with normal people, then at least they can keep up the appearance of knowing what they are doing and being aware of their actions.

Yet stakeholders just want to know one thing: "What the heck happened to my requirements?" So the next log the designers have to keep is the one containing relations between the design decisions and the requirements issued. A paragraph in a design on the generation of an error log file in HTML on some server should be linked to have an "easy-to-access medium to verify incorrect responses of export to the other system." That last is an example of a requirement. In preparation for one of the feedback meetings, a designer only has to see who's coming, extract their requirements, and present the information on what was done with them. That's feedback especially tailored to suit you.

As a closing remark for this section, remember that designing is an iterative process; you design, you discuss, you throw stuff away, and then you put new considerations into it. You win some, you lose some. Keep this in mind when you design the process to perform these activities. Brooks even states that you have to plan to throw one away, because you will in the end, anyway.[3]

Get It Signed

Once in a while, we have these live debates among our government officials on television (remember, I'm Dutch). It's a rare chance to see democracy in action. Party A states something. Party B is "in principle not negative in respect to the suggestion." Party C "can imagine an agreement with consideration of aspects that are currently not known but could arise in the future possibly, or not at all." You watch this soap opera and you think they all agree. You think wrong. Weeks later, they have the same discussion and you have the idea that they don't agree. Wrong. They do. Do they? And after four years of discussion, we get a new government.

Have you ever been at a meeting where at some point during the proceedings you are quite sure that you know where the other guy stands? You think that you know exactly what his opinion is. You walk out of the room, you drive home, and you reflect on the meeting and realize you can't remember even one exact statement that supports your feeling. If you haven't experienced this yet, just do a software project and you soon will.

Get It Signed!

It's very important that the stakeholders get the feedback from the designers, but it is at the same level of importance that the project manager get the feedback that the stakeholders were happy (or unhappy) with what they saw. Don't forget that you, the software project manager, are also a stakeholder, and you should also take care of your stakes.

You have to make sure you make progress within the project and that small steps are taken in the right direction, and you must have this feedback in an indisputable way. You just have to get it signed!

After presenting some feedback to the stakeholders, let them sign that they agree on what they saw and that what they saw takes care of their requirements. If they state, "That's a nice design," your answer has to be, "That's nice, now please sign here." If people are forced to make a formal commitment on a piece of paper (or electronic equivalent of paper), they read more carefully before they commit, and after signing they stick to their statement longer. It's not a matter of cost (we will handle that in the next section), but it's a way of getting some stable points in an otherwise dynamic (or chaotic) environment.

Get It Signed!

Of course, the procedure for what to sign should be in relation to the size of the project. It doesn't make sense to sign every paragraph, but don't wait until the end when everything is ready. Get intermediate approvals. In some weird way, most people are reluctant to put their commitments on paper. It's just a signature, but the request for it alone can be considered an insult. "My word should be good enough for you." Well, actually, it shouldn't. Never trust a used car salesman who says, "Trust me." If you can't get a good approval structure in place, leave the project and go home, because you will lose in the end. Everyone will bend and twist and everything will move consistently, with

186

the exception of you. Remember, you are a stakeholder, so take care of your own stakes.

While you are in this process, just think of one thing: *GET IT SIGNED*!

Giving It a Try

I sometimes ask myself disturbing questions like, *If you know the software business and you know how systems are built, are you now comfortable sitting in this airplane 10 kilometers up in the sky, flying on systems that some software geezer constructed?* Uhhh, honestly, I don't know. The best thing is not to think about it too much. What I know is this: after (or even while) designs are made, software engineers have to try things out. They are not always sure that certain concepts can be carried out at all, or they wonder how something will act in reality. To stay with the language used in this course, they need feedback on the parts and principles they are supposed to implement. And these trials are not always thrown away . . .like they should be.

Pilots, Prototypes, and Hollywood

Frederick P. Brooks Jr. has a very clear opinion on this matter:

> The management question, therefore, is not whether to build a pilot system and throw it away. You will do that [...] Delivering that throwaway to customers buys time, but only at the cost of agony for the user, distraction for the builders while they do the redesign,

and a bad reputation for the product that the best redesign will find hard to live down.[3]

You will create pilots for trying things out, but the pilots are focused on the particular aspects that they are attempting to prove. They are *not* designed as a part of a whole, which makes them a nightmare to use in a complete system.

But before throwing them away, remember that these exercises are crucial for your project. At an early stage, they provide the first glimpses of the requirements of a product. If you take a trip to Hollywood, you should visit Universal Studios. There you can be guided through the various studios, and you will see all those little streets featured in movies and TV series. Just by standing before a building, you can appreciate the look and feel, and you can sense the ambience. If you turn the corner, you see that the street consists of only the front of the houses. Disappointed? No. The mock-ups serve their purpose.

A prototype is a mock-up of software, a Hollywood system. You can use it in an early stage to give users a sense of what the end product will look like. Mostly it's just a window with buttons that don't do anything, but users can mentally walk through the system. Don't forget to tell them it's a mock-up, to avoid later disappointments. Feedback time! And if they like it, get it signed!

Proof of Concept and Benchmarks

A couple of years ago, I did a project where we implemented a system that consisted of multiple remote databases that had to be synchronized. Perhaps for you that is peanuts, but at that time we had no experience in this concept. Okay, it was done elsewhere, so it had to be possible. The supplier of the software had done a small exercise in this area with an administrative system that was used internally for tracking the projects. It consisted of one central database and small databases on the engineers' laptops. This provided a perfect feedback to the customer that the concept could be done, a so-called *proof of concept*.

However, skepticism arose on the scalability of the concept. It might perform well with a few users and some data, but how would it perform with heavy data traffic and hundreds of users? This matter was handled by building a pilot (!) that just synchronized databases with a lot of data and a simulated workload of a user making updates and queries. The time it took for results to come back for the simulated user and the time it took to synchronize (and some other technical measurements) were used as a reference for the future system. It was considered a *benchmark*. Those measurements on the pilot were acceptable, so the system to be built was regularly checked against the benchmark. It provided feedback on the scalability and on how far away the actual system was from the acceptable measurements.

Plan It

The activities described in this section will be performed. It is how software people must work, and it is how you can provide proper feedback to your stakeholders. Listen to Brooks. Don't deliver the throwaway as a final system, or you will lose in the end. It will happen, so plan it in advance and make it an official part of your project. Schedule time to try things out; you will have to do it anyhow!

Testing

In the previous section, the main focus is on having feedback on principles, ideas, and look-and-feel samples. You need that. But it's only the start of it all. While engineers are building the system (or merely configuring it), extensive testing has to be done. Does it work and does it work properly? Perhaps you might not regard this as part of the feedback loop to the stakeholders, but consider these requirements: "It has to work" and "I don't want to reboot my system three times a day." If these requirements are explicitly stated, you are lucky. Mostly people *assume* that they speak for themselves (pity the poor fools).

Technical Testing

As a project manager, you have to be aware that testing happens. This is not just checking whether pressing the button makes the wheel spin but also ensuring that the roof is not collapsing because there happens to be some relationship between the wheel and the roof (yeah, a far-fetched example). Make sure that the parts are tested, as well as the whole of the parts. Don't trust developers if they say they don't need testing ("Software is like a banana: it ripens at the customer's"). It's a complex task and the discipline is just a few decades old. By the way, it is a discipline that starts at the level of the individual developer.

Functional Testing

This technical stuff is all fine, but what happens if the system (or parts of it) is available from the developers? You now have to test if it is functional. Does it perform what it is supposed to perform, and in the way it is supposed to perform it? It is the big final feedback to the stakeholders, and to do it properly you have to prepare in advance. Think of the real-life situation of the system in the future and come up with some scenarios that can be considered as archetype situations. Try to write scenarios (including human aspects and handling) that cover all the major aspects.

When testing an editorial system for newspapers (the big word processors on steroids), role-play is used to construct all archetype pages, including the aspects of someone writing, someone correcting, and so on. This is the big acceptance test. You therefore need to construct the scenarios with all stakeholders concerned. If the system passes the test, they just have to sign for final acceptance.

Rolling with the Punches

In this chapter, I described the pandemonium in which everyone is sharing ("Show me yours, I'll show you mine") and in general providing feedback. I discussed the need for feedback and some ways that the feedback can be given. The result of it all is change: changing requirements and the changing realization of those requirements. As I quoted before, "Unless the job has previously been done and only modest changes are needed, it is best to assume that the requirements are wrong."[16]

There are several reasons why requirements change:

- *Stakeholder Changes Mind.* By discussing and reflecting on the subject, a stakeholder can change his mind on what he wants.

- *Project Team Interprets Requirements Differently Than Intended by Stakeholder.* Two people don't understand each other.

- *"Forgotten" Requirements Pop Up.* During the project intake and the requirements determination, the scope is determined and the initial requirements are written down. In this process, you can forget one or two requirements that appear during the feedback phase.

- *Changes in the Project Surroundings Affect Project.* Things that happen outside the project can directly affect the project, like a merger or reorganization, a new policy for buying supplies,

192

a new law, or the like. The fluctuation in the surroundings can change requirements, and the longer a project runs, the more vulnerable it is to this type of change.

The software project manager has to roll with the punches. These changes are a fact of project life, so you have to deal with them. However, to be able to construct something, requirements should be relatively stable, at least long enough to build and test something.

This stability can be forced by not allowing changes to the requirements so that they are frozen. Requirements in a project will have alternating periods of change and freeze, and it's the role of the project manager to manage this process. It's called *change control:* the process by which a change is proposed, evaluated, approved or rejected, scheduled, and tracked. The key issue is to install a change control procedure that forces people to go to one central point of entry for the project; for instance, project management will decide if a change in the set of requirements is accepted or rejected. Only one person is allowed to change the set of requirements.

CHAPTER NINE

Feedback on the Process

In October of 2000, I went to the United States for the first time. Together with my then-girlfriend, I flew to Las Vegas for a month's trip into Nevada and California. We married in Las Vegas and afterwards hit the road towards Reno, Nevada. I had spoken to a lot of people before we took the trip, and they told me, "You can drive there for hours and not see anyone." Being from western Europe, I thought, *Yeah, sure, right.*

In my area, the best you can do is not to see anyone for ten minutes in the neighborhood of nuclear waste disposals. So I hit the road, Jack. Rental car, newlywed wife next to me, climate control to the max, Rick James funkin'

195

from the CD player, driving through Nevada. You know those postcards where you just see a road going straight to the horizon and then disappearing, with nothing but nature all around it? That's what I got for two days.

When they said, "nothing," they really meant *nothing*. Most of the time, I had no idea how far I had gone or how much time I needed to find a town consisting of more than two houses and get some gas. It was just this one road, and once in a very long while you hit upon a landmark (like an old mine), and I was able to determine, "Okay, honey, we can go to the bathroom within two to four hours." The advantage of traveling on only one road is that you cannot go wrong: no exits, no decisions, no errors.

Driving from Las Vegas to Reno is easy compared to driving from my hometown to a customer I once worked for. It's only 50 kilometers in distance but full of twists and turns, detours, and uncharted roads on newly-built industrial areas. Every 500 meters you have to make a decision.

Driving Miss Project

Project progress is all about driving the project on the road towards its final destination. Where are we and how long do we still have to go? Attached to the answers to these questions are the requirements of the stakeholders towards the process of the project: Are we still within budget? Will we make it on time?

The *project progress* is an indicator relative to the path from the start to the estimated end. It's an indicator of where you are on this path, and it's always a comparison between two situations; for example, the start and the end. *Project status,* on the other hand, is a description of a certain moment in time, a snapshot of a particular situation. Status is "We spent $300" and progress is "We have now spent 40% of our total budget and we are on 30% of the total duration."

Feedback All Over Again

I hope you first read the previous chapter on requirements validation. There the issue was giving feedback on the product requirements. In this section the mantra is, "giving feedback on process requirements." And frankly, the experience is that this particular feedback loop is the more appreciated one. It's high profile, so if you really succeed in this one, your career is set. So it's a good way of helping your own stakes.

In this chapter, I talk about schedules and budgets, simply because it's the way to communicate the feedback on the project progress. I will even go so far as to yap a little about Gantt, not because Gantt *is* project management but just for the fact that it's an accepted way of communicating; most of the time it's even because some stakeholders do believe Gantt *is* project management, and it's always easier to communicate within the expectations of the other party.

But remember, it's feedback time all over again.

This type of feedback is in its diversity easier than the product feedback:

- For the subject, you can choose among time, cost, quality, and scope (with the first two as the main events)

- You either provide a progress overview or some statement about the status

- The remaining subjects are:

    - The frequency at which you provide the feedback

    - The medium used (spoken or written)

    - The level of detail

It has less diversity, but enough to fill a chapter.

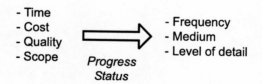

Figure 9-1: Aspects to Consider When Providing Feedback on the Process

Schedule

If you check your bank account, it's not because you want to see just the numbers; I assume that you are not a kind of number fetishist that gets his or her kicks from watching numbers on a piece of paper (if you are, then these are especially for you: 633677290 . . . oooh, aaah). By knowing the state of your finances, you can determine how much you can still buy, how much you can give away to charity, and so on. It provides you with information on how much you can satisfy your own stakes.

The project progress provides information for the stakeholders who issued requirements to the process, or to the way the project is conducted. Although I encountered some financial people that come very close to fetishism, keep in mind during this entire section that it's not the numbers that are important but the impact of the numbers on the stakes.

Road to Nowhere

To determine the progress, in time and in money, you have to have some roadmap. For time, this is a *schedule,* and for money this is a *budget.* The schedule itself is not that difficult: it's a list of tasks, start and end dates, who will perform the tasks, what will be the effort. Getting the schedule is something else, but, as with everything in this course, it's not rocket science. A good starting point for creating the schedule is the project strategy you created during the intake. You have some phases and you now need to fill in these phases with some details. And that's where the WBS comes in.

WBS does not stand for What BS. Well, sometimes it does, but normally it's a *work breakdown structure*. You take a piece of paper and you write on top of it the tasks you must perform. Under that, you write the tasks that make up this higher task; it's actually a detailed breakdown of the first task. And you can do this for every task, resulting in a nice tree-shaped structure of tasks.

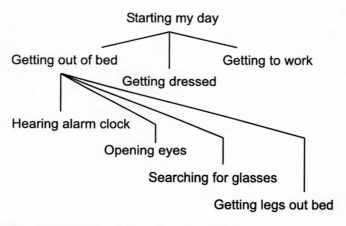

Figure 9-2: Work Breakdown Structure (WBS)

How far in detail should you go? There is no definitive answer to this question. There should be enough detail to provide you with insight into the tasks that have to be performed, but not to the level of tasks that will take two hours to perform. That kind of detail is too much, and it can even knock the flexibility out of your approach if during the project you find out you forgot something or things are not going as you anticipated. This is a mistake encouraged by some stakeholders who are happy to see a WBS of 15 pages or more, taking it as an indication that the project manager has anticipated everything.

I read this comment from a project manager somewhere:

> My personal rule of thumb is this: If I can't fit the key tasks and milestones on a regular-sized sheet of paper and still read it, it's time to delegate part of the planning.

Milestones or Millstones?

With the phases and the WBS, you can construct a list of tasks to be performed. Picking the dates for the tasks is an estimation problem, which we will handle later on. How do you handle a list of tasks? How do you control the schedule? The answer is to have *milestones*.

Milestones are events with a specific date in the schedule that function like a kind of beacon. They represent a state of the project that is unambiguous. Either you are there or you are not there. You know those computer games where you have to race and pass all these checkpoints within a certain time frame? In a project, we call them milestones. Actually, all there is to say about milestones is in the following quote from Frederick P. Brooks Jr.:

> For picking the milestones there is only one relevant rule. Milestones must be concrete, specific, measurable events, defined with knife-edge sharpness. Coding for a counterexample is '90 percent

201

finished' for half of the total coding time. Debugging is
'99 percent complete' most of the time. 'Planning
complete' is an event one can proclaim almost at will.

Concrete milestones, on the other hand, are 100-
percent events. 'Specifications signed by architects and
implementers,' 'source coding 100 percent complete,
keypunched, entered into disk library,' 'debugged
version passes all test cases.' These concrete
milestones demark the vague phases of planning,
coding, debugging.[3]

Budget

The Europeans discovered America by accident. When they
sailed over the ocean, they suddenly stumbled upon some
land. The first time they encountered the native inhabitants,
they used rum to keep from being scalped. On their next
journey, they came prepared. They brought beans and
mirrors to trade with the Indians.

So the Europeans generously gave Indians the
mirrors and other colorful, shiny trinkets in exchange for the
land. However, there was so much land and so many tribes
to encounter that they had no idea how much to take with
them. After some experience, the Spanish, Portuguese, and
Dutch travelers could give a good estimate of how much to
bring with them to take all the land. They even evolved
some kind of metric: five beans for five square miles of land.
The confiscation of land took a pace never seen before.
Later on, they discovered that they could not bring all the
beans and mirrors they needed, so they took guns instead.

The less important lesson history is trying to teach us here is that if you come prepared, you are more efficient.

Show Me the Money

To be able to give some statement on the financial state of a project, you first have to get a clue about the expected total amount you will spend and learn where your costs are. Which parts of your project require money?

To create such an overview or to check an already existing one, you should take the WBS you constructed for the project. For every task (or group of tasks), you determine who will do it and what is needed (in material) to do the job. An example is: "Programming the interface will be done by Dick and he will need a PC, a programming environment, and a room to work in." For each person and type of material, you need the units (man day, square feet, etc.) and the cost per unit. For the previous example, you can get the following table:

Item	Amount	Unit	Cost/Unit	Total
Dick	5	Day	$1000	$5000
PC	1	Piece	$2000	$2000
Programming environment	1	Piece	$899	$899
A room	20	Square feet	$10	$200

For your budget, you have to cluster the costs that are similar in type, such as hardware, software, infrastructure, personnel project costs (you know, the cost of Dick and the like), and training. This is to avoid having 20 pages of costs to get an overview of the budget; it's a kind of summary.

Telling Time

How long would it take you to walk the marathon? If someone asked me this question, am I able to answer it? I never walked 42 kilometers, but I think I could answer anyway. I once completed half a marathon, so I have some indication (believe me, this was years ago). I would just multiply that time by two and add a little bit. So, although I didn't do the job previously, I can give a reasonable estimation on the duration.

How long would it take to make your own dress? If someone asked me this question, I am in trouble. First, I would be worried by the question itself, and second, even if I tried, I would be unable to give you a proper estimate. I would know how to make a small website. I would know how to make an excellent spaghetti dinner. My best guess would be something in between the site and the pasta.

Yep, we are now talking all about estimating. So pick up the dice, and start rolling them . . .

Getting an Estimate

You already created a nice WBS and put some millstones (just kidding, milestones) in them. That's just fine. It is a nice structure, but it tells you nothing about the most important part of a schedule, time. Someone has to yell out some dates. How long will it take, when can you start?

The best people to provide you with an estimate are the people who will have to perform the tasks. First of all, they probably know what they are talking about, but most of all, it will be their estimation. Otherwise, if you have to work with the people later on in the project and you provided the estimate, normally they will not agree and will not feel committed to doing the work in your estimated time instead of theirs. Getting a good estimate from, let's say, a programmer is not just a task for the programmer himself. The project manager plays a critical role in getting quality numbers. He has to talk with the guy (or gal) to see why the estimate is that it will take seven days. It's because he already walked half a marathon or because he thinks a dress and spaghetti are the same to create. I know, I repeat myself. I already stated this before, but just do it, for cryin' out loud.

So the project manager is a kind of shrink for the programmers. That's right. They just have to kick back and say what comes to their minds, and that's it. Yeah, right, duh! The programmer, in this case, should take steps to ensure that his estimates are getting more and more accurate. He can do this by keeping statistics on how much time he spends on each task, how accurate his previous estimates were, and so on.

I dug up this quote on an Internet newsgroup:

My experience is that people work to deadlines. If an engineer estimates a task will take 4 weeks, they do *not* mean 4x40=160 Hrs. They mean it's feasible that it will be done 4 weeks after the start, and the Engineer will put in as many or few hours as necessary to get it done. One [sic] one hand, the Engineer will be factoring in such things as other workloads going on, planned days off, etc. On the other, most people will underestimate the time it actually takes, and the experienced manager will know how to 'pad' (or in some cases shrink) the estimate based on the track record of the individual.[20]

Gantt and Pert: Great Graphs

If you take all your tasks from the WBS and you estimate how long they will take and when they will start and finish, you have the ammunition to create one of the icons of project management: the Gantt Chart. It is a good way to visualize the information you have before you. And because it's considered an icon, using it in your communication will put some stakeholders at ease. Basically, Gantt is an overview of tasks. You put weeks, days, or months at one side, and the tasks at the other. You draw fat lines to indicate the periods in which the tasks will be performed.

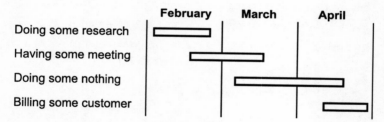

Figure 9-3: Gantt Chart Sample

Next to the task, put the name of the person who will do the job, and you come a long way.

206

PERT: Almost as Good as Gantt

If Sesame Street has Bert and Ernie, project management has
PERT and Gantt. PERT is a notation technique that has a lot
of fun features I will not discuss. The good thing about
creating a PERT chart is that you have to think about the
relations between tasks. Can Task X start before Task Y?
Do they have to end together? Must they start at the same
time? You get the idea. If you think in this way about your
tasks, you can create graphs like the one shown below.

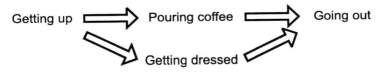

Figure 9-4: PERT Chart Sample

Before you can pour your coffee, you have to wake
up. Before you can get dressed, you have to be up. You
don't have to be dressed to pour the coffee. However, you
have to be dressed and finished with your coffee before you
can leave for the office.

Suppose "pouring coffee" takes you 5 minutes and
"getting dressed" takes 15 minutes. Suppose your wife pours
your coffee. In that case, the time it will take you to get up
and leave home is the total time for "getting up" + "getting
dressed" + "going out." Let's say that it comes to 30
minutes. As long as your wife stays under the 15 minutes, you
have no delay. Only if she decides to make you an espresso,
you are late. You see why? This is very useful information, not

for the example I used, but for the project you have to take on. It shows you who has to wait for whom and stuff like that. It shows that a delay of one task does not automatically mean a delay of the entire project. All the tasks that have this property, however, are called the *critical path*. These activities have to be done sequentially and will take the longest in that time frame, and a delay in one of the tasks within the critical path will cause a delay in the entire project.

Tardis Wallpaper

> This isn't a project plan, it's wallpaper for the Tardis you're going to need to meet these ^&*&%*& timescales"[21]

Why is it a programmer has these success stories on how he constructed in his free time the most incredible foo-compiler within two days, and without bugs? Why is it that the same programmer cannot finish a simple dialog for a payroll system within the agreed period—a period he himself indicated (and which, by the way, he grossly exaggerated)? If it isn't going to happen anyway, why does a project manager bother planning programmers?

Okay, the previous paragraph is meant in a provocative manner, but being a software project manager, you will have these questions cross your mind. And of course, there's another view on the subject, the one from the perspective of the programmer:

> Why do I have the following discussion over and over
> with the project manager: 'I told you it would take 3
> weeks, so why did you cut it to 2 weeks, just because
> it met the quarter reporting deadline? Why do I have
> to tell you 'your $%^&^ plan bears so little relation to
> the Babylonian calendar that the rest of the world uses
> that you must be a ^%%&*' Mayan?'[21]

I know why I need a planning. It is a useful tool to communicate the tasks, time scales, and dependencies within a project. It's a way to indicate the agreements with several parties on when this or that is ready. But why should programmers be bothered with a planning? What are the effects of their handing over a Gantt chart? Is it the right way to communicate anyway? What does a programmer want from a planning?

So, on an Internet discussion forum I posted this simple question: "Why does a programmer need a schedule or a budget?"[22] This section reflects some of the answers and, of course, more strongly, my personal view on the matter.

I will use the terms "planning" and "schedule" interchangeably in this section. Actually, a planning can be a larger document with backgrounds, etceteras, and a schedule (tasks, person, time). However, large documents are never read, and everyone just goes straight for the schedule. So, in most cases just the schedule is provided. That's why we can use the terms, for the sake of this section, for the same item.

Agreement

When I order some furniture in Holland, the guys who will deliver the stuff to my home send me a letter indicating which day they will come to my doorstep. The day for them starts at 8 a.m. and ends at 10 p.m., so I take a day off and I wait. And I sit. And I sit and wait. Sitting and waiting is not my favorite waste of time, especially on the job (I'm a fanatic, what can I say). For the projects I run, I will have some kind of planning, so I know when I can get my stuff to bring to the next guy. This next guy is also glad that I can tell him exactly when he gets the stuff he needs to do his thing. All in all, from my planning I can tell a lot of stories.

My storyboard in this respect might be a Gantt chart. I can send this chart to a fellow project manager, and he will immediately know what I mean. I also use the chart to put in when a certain programmer performs a specific task and how long it takes. I do this to put our mutual agreement in writing. "How long will it take and when will it be ready?" "Well, it takes one week and I start on Monday." The Gantt will be used to tell the programmer that I consent to what we agreed on and to let the rest of the world in on our little secret.

So that's why I, a software project manager, send the programmer the planning in the first place. Why do I need a written agreement, and can't I be satisfied with just a telephone call? I wasn't even aware of that question, let alone the answer, but those responding to my online query certainly were. I'm playing devil's advocate here, but the following paragraph summarizes how some programmers feel about the whole subject of planning.

You need a schedule for the programmer; otherwise, he will never do the job you ask of him. A typical programmer would rather be writing a compiler than creating a non-challenging, dull dialog for the payroll system. So, if you let him schedule his own stuff (or no planning at all), he will probably do the things he really likes first, like internetting, chatting, or taking the kids to the zoo. If you approach this pessimistically, issuing a schedule is the only way to provide the project manager with some power. Non-delivery of a product is something that can be easily proven, so a written planning is therefore a perfect form of surveillance of the programmer. And this type of monitoring is needed. Otherwise, the programmer just slacks off.

I'm not completely happy with this form of reasoning because it's too darn cynical, but if we are looking for a short statement on reality, this one is fairly close to it. I want to communicate to the programmer our agreement. This is still the case. I'm only wondering if providing a Gantt chart to a programmer is such a smart move. I'm curious about how I would respond if he answers me with something in UML or Bachus/Naur form.

What's This Thing Called a Planning?

The software project manager walks into the room, very proud, handing over his new, fresh Gantt chart. It's shiny. The programmer looks at it. He holds it up to the light. The project manager wonders what the programmer is thinking.

How do I read this? What is this? The more experienced programmer goes straight to the second thought: *What happened to my numbers? I told him it would take 3 months; why did he slash it to 1?*

Actually, this may not be a surprise if you think of the planning as a written agreement. The programmer first looks to see if it might have been changed, and by only one party. The one who writes the document has the power to change the text and, sadly, the text of a schedule is very limited.

There is no explanation of why things are what they are or why the estimate has changed. Decreasing someone's estimates of his own tasks is a bad suggestion in the first place.

The handing over of the planning is the first form of feedback from the project manager on what he actually did with the estimates the programmer provided him earlier. If they're the same, the manager gains some credibility; if not, he's lost forever.

Does this large chart provide some use for the programmer, besides just the line with his own tasks? Yes, it does. It can provide insight into the quality of preparations for his tasks. The tasks that come after his work are not of much interest, but the past, what happened before, is key. As more evidence in support of the essential need for planning and scheduling, consider one programmer's description of what happens when this stage of the process is neglected:

> The result [of having no planning or schedule] is that when I have to do some work, I loose [sic] a lot of time getting the preparations (that have been 'forgotten' to take place), talking to people to convince [them that] I need the results NOW, doing things myself because the right person has other priorities, etcetera. And the result of that is that other people come to me wanting results *NOW* for work I didn't know I had to do.[23]

I wish that I could say, "We can throw the planning out of the Tardis, we don't need this thing." Sadly, we do need it. It's a way to communicate an agreement. However, should this way be plotted on A1 with only a Gantt chart? I don't think so. I hate these charts, anyway.

Stating Costs

You will need to talk with financial guys, so I now spend a section on higher mathematics. Remember Dick? He was part of the budget to program some application, and he was supposed to spend five days, with a total cost of $5000.

Suppose we arrange for Dick to start on Monday and he is scheduled to finish after five days on Friday. If you want to monitor the cost for Dick's endeavor, you need to monitor just the value of the *budget*: $5000, which is what is

213

originally estimated. By the way, a complete budget that is agreed upon by the customer is called a *baseline*. The budget might change due to discussions and new insight, but the baseline can only change with a signature of the customer. On Wednesday, Dick spends three days working on the stupid thing, so at that time the costs in reality are $1000 X 3 = $3000. This is the *actual cost*.

Dick's manager could now yell, "The job is 60% completed!" However, the correct phrase is, "We have now used 60% of what we originally thought (budgeted)." Looking at the bits Dick produced reveals that he has only done 25% of the application. So actually the cost should be 25% of $5000 (total budget of Dick) = $1250. In advanced project manager lingo, this value is called the *earned value*.

What is the progress? Well, 25% of the total work to be done, and used 60% of the budget and estimated time. The questions that have to be answered are: How much will it cost in the end? When is it actually finished? Dick will say that he will work harder and make up the time. He probably will, but not so much that the difference between budget and actual cost will vanish.

Enter the *Estimate at Completion* (EAC). This is a forecast of total project costs based upon how the project is currently doing, the project performance. It's something you have to calculate, preferably with a computer. EAC is calculated by taking the total budget and dividing it by a performance factor (the cost performance index, which is earned value actual cost). This assumes that the percentage by which the project has overrun today is going to be the same percentage that it overruns at completion.

So, for Dick on this Wednesday, the following overview holds:

Actual cost:	$3000
Total budget:	$5000
Earned value:	$1250
Cost performance index:	0.417.

And this brings us to an EAC of: $5000 / 0.417 = $11,990.41.

Dick's in trouble.

Taking It like a Man

Now you can create nice spreadsheets with indices and draw tree structures that resemble your tasks, and what does this bring you? First of all, it brings you acceptance as a project manager. Project managers are supposed to create such things. Many customers are not happy when their project managers don't show up with an Incredible Gantt Chart (preferably printed on A3 and double-sided).

Financial people want to see the numbers. What does it cost me in the end? They want to know as soon as possible. You can hit them now with the EAC. And, of course, the techniques are okay; they help you structure your mind, your information overload, and your life. Project progress reporting is only a nice job if you take care that the expectations of the stakeholders are in line with the current situation. There is no such thing as good news or bad news. If you run over budget, that's bad news. If you stay under budget, for most companies that's also bad news. If you are a supplier and your consultants do the job in less time than expected, you also make less profit than expected; hence, you get pissed stakeholders.

Extra Pot of Gold

Again, like the entire message of this book, take care of the stakes. It's not just the numbers; it's the consequences of what they represent that causes negative reactions of stakeholders. With budgets, the guy or gal responsible always has to defend changes to a higher level. Consider a system that will be built for a certain Business Unit A. Parts of the system being built for them will later be used by five other business units. At the start of the project, Business Unit A has a budget for the complete system. Of course, it runs out of budget. Supplier and customer are rolling over the floor with "It's your fault" and "No, it's your fault" and the like. No one wants to defend the overrun to the higher level in the company.

Suddenly, someone suggests taking out of the original budget the costs for the parts of the system that will also be used by other business units and creating an additional "pot of gold" for it. After all, it's not fair that this one business unit pays all the costs all by itself. Applause. This is something they can defend to a higher level. Their budget remains unchanged (with no overrun) and a new budget is created. The numbers remain the same and the fact that more money will be spent than originally anticipated also remains unchanged, but this is fair and no one loses face. Yep, I was there. It was not my suggestion, sadly.

Extra Tasks

Imagine that in your project schedule you have planned for testing. Some stakeholders are highly committed to the deadlines for your schedule (they probably promised someone else). Your system will not be ready for testing on this time frame, at least not the entire system. You can propose to keep the deadline for testing and add an additional task after it called "integral testing" or "test it again, Sam." The stakeholders can keep their word (they only said, "Testing will be finished") and you have your extra time. I am not claiming this works all the time. I'm just showing that you should be creative in the negotiation on budget and schedule.

CHAPTER TEN

Epilogue

Do you remember our friend Hank from the Introduction in Chapter 1? Do you think his project week would have started off a lot better if he had spent the weekend reading this book instead of kicking back and enjoying a brewskie? We may never know for sure, but at the very least this book would have spared him all those surprises during his first few days on the project.

Theories and methods paint a structured and orderly picture of project life, but as Hank quickly discovered, reality bites. And with every nibble, reality may seem farther and farther away from what the theories have led you to expect. This doesn't mean that the methods and theories have no purpose, because they truly do. Just remember that they offer an oversimplified version of reality, to make it easier for us to remember the methods. Reality is way too complex for us to stuff all of it into our heads.

So what if Hank *had* spent some time that weekend digesting all the material written on these pages? What would he have picked up from these ideas to use in his project?

The two major concepts addressed in this book are:

1. The Flow Of Stakes

2. Project Potion

The Flow Of Stakes

The most important aspect is the mindset of the project manager. He should focus on one simple mental image of the jobs he has to perform instead of trying to cram 500 pages of charting and calculating into his head. He should know the flow of stakes:

- • Stakeholders have stakes

- • Stakeholders communicate their stakes by expressing their expectations, and these are more formally defined by means of requirements to the process or product

- • Project management should make every stakeholder a winner by accepting and creating requirements that continually satisfy the stakes of individual stakeholders and do not conflict with the general process or the product

- Project management should give continuous feedback to the stakeholders on the state of the stakes

- Based upon this feedback, the expectations and requirements might change, and in this way a new cycle begins

For a lot of people involved in projects, one inescapable conclusion still comes as a big surprise: project management is a *people* business. It's all about keeping everyone associated with the project happy by supporting his or her stakes. The trouble with stakes is that no one tells you what they are. You have to guess, negotiate, anticipate, and manipulate to get past the requirements and directly through to the fears and wishes of people. Software project management is more about psychology than technology.

Project Potion

Different project circumstances require different approaches to ensure optimum effectiveness. As mentioned above, it is the people who largely determine these circumstances, and you have to tailor your software approach to the particular situation. For this you can make use of techniques and tools from different existing methods by simply mixing and matching everything together in such a way that you brew the right Project Potion for the occasion.

Concocting a Project Potion consists of the following steps:

221

1. You analyze the stakeholders and their interests and expectations (Stakeholder Analysis).

2. You analyze the products (technical stuff) you have to create.

3. You determine the potential risks that might exist (Risk Management).

4. You create a project approach that reduces those risks, and for this you have three main tools:

   - *Strategy*: What are the steps taken in the project, and what are the sequence and time frame?

   - *Organization*: How is your project organization constructed?

   - *Feedback*: How is the feedback to the stakeholders on the status and content of products and processes organized?

The Future for Hank

Hank will come a long way with these concepts, but to take full advantage of the potential in the material presented, he will have to take his study a little further. He will need to look at existing project management and software development methods and find approaches he can use on his own project. Precisely for this purpose, I provide in the following "Appendix: Using Methods" section some recommended starting points to existing methods for further study.

Always keep in mind that no book, not even this one, offers a recipe for instant project management success. There is no magic pill that you can take to make all your project troubles vanish into thin air. Software project management achieved through the Flow of the Stakes and the Project Potion is a stakeholder-oriented state of mind, a way of life. To derive the most benefit out of these concepts, you must have the commitment and discipline to put them into action. Once you do that, you will find that it is well worth the effort.

Using Methods

The idea that there is no single right way to perform software projects is not new. Plan-driven methods like PMP and Prince2 indicate that you most likely have to scale them down and not just use everything the method provides. Alistair Cockburn's Crystal Family of methods assumes that for different projects you have to use a different member of the family, depending on aspects like size, quality, and speed. A method like Scrum provides extra attention to the fact that it can be effectively used in combination with other approaches within a project.

In *Balancing Agility and Discipline: A Guide for the Perplexed and Agile and Iterative Development*, Barry W. Boehm and Richard Turner[7] devote an entire book to reaching a sweet spot for your project, the right mix of agile and plan-driven methods. How much more tailored to your situation can your approach get?

These are just samples of the method gurus, but in reality, if you look at the good, very senior project managers, you see something similar happening. I have been working within software projects for over a decade. I have worked with some very good (and, of course, also some very bad) project managers. The very good ones assess the project situation, lean back, think for a while, and draw up a fabulous approach, one that is just right.

Most of the time, you will not find an exact blueprint of an approach that is sold somewhere in a bookstore. The seniors tap into their experience of what worked before and what didn't and recall things they read in the past or just heard from a colleague down the hall. "I did this and this, and the problem was fixed." They tap into their knowledge of methods, techniques, and approaches and create a nice pastry that saves the project day.

Why not? Every technique ever invented had at least one problem or situation in mind. If you encounter the same problem or circumstances, why not use the applicable method? So I am not talking about having a method that attacks different situations; my aim is more modest. Why not use the whole enchilada that is out there by just picking the parts you need, regardless of the name on the method? Thanks to the Internet, there is a lot of information right at your fingertips.

To help you get started on your voyage of method discovery, this appendix provides some samples on:

- How a technique can be useful in one case and harmful in another

- Why you shouldn't pick just any process component

- Using an agile technique in a plan-driven context

- How to "read" a real method

- A starting point to different methods

Different Circumstances, Different Effectiveness in Techniques: Big Design Up-Front

Traditional approaches (read "plan-driven") will dictate that you first specify in detail what you want, before you start building the software. In the rigid approach, where you may not code anything before the design is approved, we call this the "Big Design Up-Front."

We all know that the Big Design Up-Front (BDU) that we all used in the old days is dying out. Its purpose is to define everything that has to be built up front, so the process is nice and predictable. In the last decade, we found out that this is not such a good idea after all. The requirements change or are even unknown, so what is specified up front will be wrong, anyway. BDU, as a tool for feedback to the end users on what has to be built, is dead (or should be). The

227

lean and mean validation process of short iterations and close end user cooperation provides more promising results.

However, feedback and validation to end users is not the only purpose of BDU. The design is also used to solve risks of miscommunication between parties and can be used as a formal document (as for contracts). If you have multiple parties that are not in the same geographical location but are working in parallel on highly connected system components (like interfaces), you might need a big design in the beginning. It will function as the main source for all parties to perform their tasks.

If you are going to work in a highly political, blame-it-on-the-other-guy environment, you'd better cover your back and create a large document in the beginning describing what you are going to create, to be part of the contractual agreements.

Some professionals might have the tendency to take an attitude like, "If they can't tell me what they want, we shouldn't even bother." In theory, you should be able to get at least close to 80% on paper up front. But sometimes it is wiser to support the users in their "I know what I want when I see it" mood just to be able to proceed and to get something useful. This is better than forcing large requirements and design sessions and having binders of documents that are mostly hard to read for end users (if they read them at all).

This is a sample of how techniques can be helpful under different circumstances. Even the old techniques everybody complains about (or defends heavily) serve their purposes.

Also, the agile alternatives to BDU (iterative, close user involvement, and so on) have their risks (in no particular order, and without any intention of being complete):

- Miscommunication when there is a distance in team members in time or geographic location

- More vulnerability to changes in project team members

- Shorter planning horizon, so more difficulty in planning/estimating costs for the whole (not every customer can handle this)

- Risk of requirements inflation (end user communicates directly with developer)

Not Every Single Process Component Is Effective Alone: Iterations

Although I propose picking different techniques and process components from every method that you can lay your hands on, this doesn't mean that you can just pick a single piece from a method and hope it will work.

I stress that an issue should be tackled by the introduction of a certain process component. A certain risk should be reduced. So sometimes this means that you have to add another piece in tandem with the technique you had in mind. They go hand in hand, and one without the other would be useless.

229

Alistair Cockburn provides a nice example in his article, "Are Iterations Hazardous to Your Project?" (http://alistair.cockburn.us/crystal/articles/aih/areiterationshazardous.htm).[24] Simply doing iterations in development without involving the users in the intermediate results is just wasting your time. Iterations are intended as a feedback mechanism; just iterating without the feedback part will make the techniques ineffective. In the words of Cockburn, "Danger grows when the results of the iteration are not directly linked to delivering the product to the end user."[24]

You Can Mix and Match: Burn-Down Chart Instead of Gantt

Just to reassure you: yes, you can use different techniques together. I will take as an example the usage of burn-down charts as described for Crystal Clear. However, this technique can also be found elsewhere, as in Scrum and Extreme Programming.

A burn-down chart is a chart that reflects the progress made on development. It will list the number of features on the y-axis and the time on the x-axis. As time progresses, the line should go down.

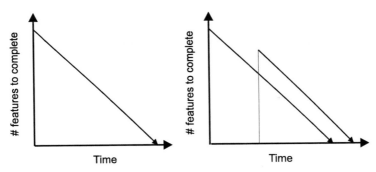

Figure A-1: Burn-Down Chart and Burn-Down Chart after Scope Increase (after Cockburn, 2005)[27]

In more plan-driven methods, an updated Gantt chart can be used to indicate the progress. However, I like the simplicity and effectiveness in communication of this style of chart. In one clear image it says it all about the progress of development.

Another nifty thing is that you can indicate scope increase in a clear manner (second chart in the figure). If you are on a tight deadline but users keep on adding requirements (scope increase), you can just up the line for the number of features left to complete and draw a new estimate line. By leaving the original line in the chart, you make it very clear to the sponsors that you are running late because of the increase in scope.

Regardless of which method you use, even if plan-driven like PMP and Prince 2, you can use this method of communication.

Method Components Have a Reason: Scrum (Sample)

Suppose that after reading this book you encountered a "real" method. How would you handle the information provided? To help you out on this matter, I created this small sample using Scrum, and I turn to some global observations about it. I use the word "global" as I will not go into every little detail, but use the information that is available on the fabulous site ControlChaos.com.

Taken from that site:

Scrum's Three Tools

1. Backlog: Overall, by product line, by product, and by system an organization identifies all outstanding work and prioritizes it. This prioritized backlog list changes continuously and is updated and re-prioritized continuously.

2. Sprints: Work increments where a team works on completing an identified, self-contained group of prioritized work. During the sprint, the work is not changed from outside the sprint, although as work occurs in the sprint, additional work may be uncovered.

3. Scrums: Daily meetings where a Sprint team meets to identify what work was just done, what work will be done next, and what is impeding work. [25]

Here are some of my observations to add to the information given above:

1. **Backlog**: This list is the general planning tool. This is needed to provide feedback to the team members on what should be done, feedback to the users on what will be happening with their requirements, and feedback to management on progress and need for interventions/decisions. As only the items are planned for the current and/or next sprint (iteration), it can cause a problem with management that wants to have some statement about the long-term planning and cost. On the other hand, the underlying idea behind Scrum is that with unknown requirements (see 2. Sprints), every statement about the long term is almost useless. Only based upon the real speed of the team are time frames determined, and only for the foreseeable future. So the question is: Can you convince management that it is better to stay in reality and get involved in the process, or do they want to work with statements based upon "feelings" and "hunches" and have a false sense of security (some people prefer the latter)?

2. **Sprints**: Scrum uses an incremental approach to provide early feedback of some end result. The underlying risk that is covered here is "uncertainties in requirements." By providing feedback in a working version as early as

possible, this system allows the end users to view if the requirements are properly addressed. Also, a close involvement of end users within the Scrum team covers this risk. However, to be able to determine if the requirements are properly addressed, users will have to look to at least some version of the system that satisfies a certain business goal in its whole. As certain sets of requirements are dependent on each other, a real opinion can only be formed when a major part of the requirements are addressed.

If you look further in the sprint definition, you will find that it has to satisfy a "sprint goal," which should be some business goal. So Scrum doesn't promote iterations just for the sake of iterations. The idea is to provide feedback, and if that is not possible in a good way, the increments don't make any sense.

3. Scrums

The Daily Scrums last no more than fifteen minutes. During the meeting, everyone on the team answers three questions:

1. *What have you done since the last Daily Scrum?*

2. *What will you do between now and the next Daily Scrum?*

3. *What's getting in the way of your doing your work?*[25]

234

This is to provide daily feedback to each other (including management) on the current state of the work and to address issues that need to be taken care of. Actually, these are just rules for an efficient meeting. Other methods also provide this, but the aggressiveness of the name "Scrum" has strong appeal.

From this short sample you can see that feedback on product and process are used to either reduce risks or satisfy the needs of stakeholders. You can also use the backlog technique in approaches other than Scrum. Heck, priority lists of requirements and risks can be found in other methods also. However, calling it a "backlog" is an in-your-face name, calling it exactly what it is.

There are more methods that take an incremental or iterative approach, but always remember what it is you are trying to address, why you go incremental. Without having the "sprint goal," the sprints would be useless.

Recommended Starting Point for Other Methods

In this section, I provide a short list of methods I recommend reading up on for starters.

- **PMP**: Plan-driven method created by Project Management Institute; large user base in U.S. http://www.pmi.org

- **Prince 2**: Plan-driven method; large user base in Europe.
  http://www.ogc.gov.uk/prince2/

- **Scrum**: Agile method with focus on management aspects; not necessarily needed for software projects.
  http://www.controlchaos.com

  Recommended as introductory audio book: *Agile Project Management Using Scrum* by Kevin Aguanno.[26]

- **Crystal Clear**: A human-powered methodology for small teams (agile) created by Alistair Cockburn as part of a whole range of methods (Crystal Family).
  http://alistair.cockburn.us/
  Recommended reading: *Crystal Clear - A Human-Powered Methodology for Small Teams* by Alistair Cockburn[27]

- **DSDM**: Framework for business-centered development (agile) with very comprehensive method for software development; user base largely in Europe.
  http://www.dsdm.org

References

[1] Hoff, Benjamin. *The Tao of Pooh*. New York: Penguin
Books, 1983.

[2] Boehm, Barry W. and Rony Ross. "Theory-W Software
Project Management Principles and Examples."
IEEE Transactions on Software Engineering 15.7
(1989): 902-916.

[3] Brooks, Frederick P. Jr. *The Mythical Man-Month: Essays
on Software Engineering*. 20th anniversary ed.
Boston: Addison-Wesley Publishing, 1995.

[4] Fisher, Roger and William Ury. Ed. Bruce Patton. *Getting
to Yes: Negotiating Agreement without Giving In*. 2nd
ed. New York: Penguin Books, 1991.

5 Gray, John. *Men Are from Mars, Women Are From Venus: A Practical Guide for Improving Communication and Getting What You Want in Your Relationships.* New York: Harper Collins, 1992.

6 "Overheard at the Trial." *Wired News.* Lycos, Inc. 2 Mar 2006. <http://www.wired.com/news/antitrust/ 0,551,18715,00.html>.

7 Boehm, Barry W. and Richard Turner. *Balancing Agility and Discipline: A Guide for the Perplexed and Agile and Iterative Development: A Manager's Guide.* Boston: Addison-Wesley Publishing, 2004.

8 Boehm, Barry W. and P. Bose. *A Collaborative Spiral Software Process Model Based on Theory W.* Proc. of Third International Conference on the Software Process, Applying the Software Process. Reston, VA: IEEE, 1994.

9 Hall, Elaine M. *Managing Risk: Methods for Software Systems Development.* SEI Series in Software Engineering. Reading, MA: Addison-Wesley Publishing, 1998.

10 Humphrey, Watts S. *A Discipline for Software Engineering.* Addison-Wesley Publishing, Reading, MA: 1995.

11 D'Herbemont, Olivier and Bruno Cesar. *Managing Sensitive Projects: A Lateral Approach.* New York: Routledge, 1998.

[12] Alderfer, Clayton P. E*xistence, Relatedness and Growth: Human Needs in Organizational Settings.* New York: Free Press, 1972.

[13] "Risk Management." *Software Engineering Institute.* Carnegie Mellon University. 2006. 3 Mar 2006. <http://www.sei.cmu.edu/risk/main.html>.

[14] Carr, Marvin J. et al. "Taxonomy-Based Risk Identification." *Software Engineering Institute Technical Report.* Pittsburgh: Software Engineering Institute, 1993.

[15] Aguanno, Kevin. *Managing Agile Projects.* Ed. Kevin Aguanno. Lakefield, Ontario: Multi-Media Publications, 2005.

[16] Humphrey, Watts S. *Managing the Software Process.* Reading, MA: Addison-Wesley Publishing, 1989.

[17] Martin, James. *Rapid Application Development.* New York: MacMillan, 1991.

[18] "MoSCoW Rules." *DSDM Consortium.* Dynamic Systems Development Method, Ltd. 1994-2006. 5 Mar 2006. <http://www.dsdm.org/en/about/moscow/asp>.

[19] Cockburn, Alistair. "Structuring Use Cases with Goals." *Humans and Technology.* 2000. 1 March 2006. <http://alistair.cockburn.us/crystal/articles/sucwg/structuringucswithgoals.htm>.

[20] Bck. "Do You Plan for 40 Hour Week and Work a 60?" Online posting. 10 Jan. 2001. *Google Groups: alt.projectmng.* 3 Mar 2006. < http:// groups.google.com/group/alt.projectmng/ browse_thread/thread/1a65ae66d34eda04/ 553f3523d341406?lnk=st&rnum= 1#55c3f3523d341406 >.

[21] Dingley, Andy. "Why Does a Programmer Need a Schedule or a Budget?" Online posting. 13 Aug 2001. *Google Groups: comp.software-eng. 2 Mar 2006.* <http://groups.google.com/group/ comp.software-eng/browse_thread/thread/ 9d49153600946f71/ d5ead330231f40fd?lnk=st&rnum=8#d5ead330231f40fd>.

[22] DeBaar, Bas. "Why Does a Programmer Need a Schedule or a Budget?" Online posting. 8 Aug. 2001. *Google Groups: comp.software-eng.* 2 Mar. 2006. <http:// groups.google.com/group/comp.software- eng/ browse_thread/thread/9d49153600946f71/ d5ead330231f40fd?lnk=st&rnum=8#d5ead330231f40fd>.

[23] Sch., Frank. "Why Does a Programmer Need a Schedule or a Budget?" Online posting. 9 Aug 2001. *Google Group: comp.software-eng.* 2 March 2006. <http:// groups.google.com/group/comp.software- 600946f71/ d5ead330231f40fd?lnk=st&rnum=8#d5ead330231f40fd>.

[24] Cockburn, Alistair. "Are Iterations Hazardous to Your Project?" *Humans and Technology.* HaT TR 2005.04. 9 Sept. 2005. 1 March 2006. <http://alistair.cockburn.us/crystal/articles/aih/areiterationshazardous.htm>.

[25] "Scrum: It's About Common Sense." *Control Chaos.* 2006. 1 March 2006. <ControlChaos.com>.

[26] Aguanno, Kevin. *Agile Project Management Using Scrum.* Audio CD. Lakefield, Ontario: Multi-Media Publications, 2005.

[27] Cockburn, Alistair. *Crystal Clear: A Human-Powered Methodology for Small Teams.* Upper Saddle River, NJ: Pearson Education, 2005.

About the Author

 Bas de Baar works as a Project Manager within the publishing industry. Since 2001, he has been the editor of SoftwareProjects.org, a popular website dedicated to Software Project Management. He holds a masters degree in Business Informatics and currently lives with his wife in the coastal town of Zandvoort, The Netherlands.

Managing Smaller Projects: A Practical Approach

So called "small projects" can have potentially alarming consequences if they go wrong, but their control is often left to chance. The solution is to adapt tried and tested project management techniques.

This book provides a low overhead, highly practical way of looking after small projects. It covers all the essential skills: from project start-up, to managing risk, quality and change, through to controlling the project with a simple control system. It cuts through the jargon of project management and provides a framework that is as useful to those lacking formal training, as it is to those who are skilled project managers and want to control smaller projects without the burden of bureaucracy.

Read this best-selling book from the U.K., now making its North American debut. *IEE Engineering Management* praises the book, noting that "Simply put, this book is about helping people control smaller projects in a logical and effective way, and making the process run smoothly, and is indeed a success in achieving that goal."

Available in print format. Order from your local bookseller, Amazon.com, or directly from the publisher at **www.mmpubs.com/msp**

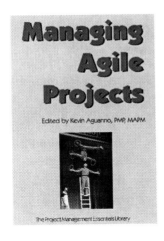

Edited by Kevin Aguanno, PMP, MAPM

The Project Management Essentials Library

Managing Agile Projects

Are you being asked to manage a project with unclear requirements, high levels of change, or a team using Extreme Programming or other Agile Methods?

If you are a project manager or team leader who is interested in learning the secrets of successfully controlling and delivering agile projects, then this is the book for you.

From learning how agile projects are different from traditional projects, to detailed guidance on a number of agile management techniques and how to introduce them onto your own projects, this book has the insider secrets from some of the industry experts – the visionaries who developed the agile methodologies in the first place.

Available in print and electronic formats. Order from your local bookseller, Amazon.com, or directly from the publisher at **www.agilesecrets.com**

Titanic Lessons for IT Projects

Titanic Lessons for IT Projects analyzes the project that designed, built, and launched the ship, showing how compromises made during early project stages led to serious flaws in this supposedly "perfect ship." In addition, the book explains how major mistakes during the early days of the ship's operations led to the disaster. All of these disasterous compromises and mistakes were fully avoidable.

Entertaining and full of intriguing historical details, this companion book to *Avoiding Project Disaster: Titanic Lessons for IT Executives* helps project managers and IT executives see the impact of decisions similar to the ones that they make every day. An easy read full of illustrations and photos to help explain the story and to help drive home some simple lessons.

Available in print and electronic formats. Order from your local bookseller, Amazon.com, or directly from the publisher at **www.mmpubs.com/titanic**

246

Project Lessons from the Great Escape (Stalag Luft III)

While you might think your project plan is perfect, would you bet your life on it?

In World War II, a group of 220 captured airmen did just that — they staked the lives of everyone in the camp on the success of a project to secretly build a series of long tunnels out of a prison camp their captors thought was escape proof.

The prisoners formally structured their work as a project, using the project organization techniques of the day. This book analyzes their efforts using modern project management methods and the nine knowledge areas from the *Guide to the Project Management Body of Knowledge* published by the Project Managment Institute. Learn from the successes and mistakes of a project where people really put their lives on the line.

Available in print and electronic formats. Order from your local bookseller, Amazon.com, or directly from the publisher at **www.mmpubs.com**

74 Tips for *Absolutely Great* Teleconference Meetings

Ida Shessel

Become a meeting superstar!

With the proliferation of teleconference meetings in today's distributed team environment, many organizations now conduct most of their meetings over the telephone instead of face-to-face. There are challenges associated with trying to ensure that these meetings are productive, successful, and well-run. Learn how to get the most out of your teleconference meetings using these practical tips.

74 Tips for Absolutely Great Teleconference Meetings contains tips for both the teleconference leader and the participant — tips on how to prepare for the teleconference, start the teleconference meeting and set the tone, lead the teleconference, keep participants away from their e-mail during the call, use voice and language effectively, and draw the teleconference to a close.

Mastering the art of holding a good meeting is one sure-fire way to get recognized as a leader by your peers and your management. Being able to hold an *absolutely great* teleconference meeting positions you as a leader who can also leverage modern technologies to improve efficiency. Develop this career-building skill by ordering this book today!

Available in electronic formats from most ebook online retailers or directly from the publisher at **www.mmpubs.com**.

Networking *for* Results

THE POWER *OF* PERSONAL CONTACT

In partnership with Michael J. Hughes, *The* Networking Guru, Multi-Media Publications Inc. has released a new series of books, ebooks, and audio books designed for business and sales professionals who want to get the most out of their networking events and help their career development.

Networking refers to the concept that each of us has a group or "network" of friends, associates and contacts as part of our on-going human activity that we can use to achieve certain objectives.

The *Networking for Results* series of products shows us how to think about networking strategically, and gives us step-by-step techniques for helping ourselves and those around us achieve our goals. By following these practices, we can greatly improve our personal networking effectiveness.

Visit **www.Networking-for-Results.com** for information on specific products in this series, to read free articles on networking skills, or to sign up for a free networking tips newsletter. Products are available from most book, ebook, and audiobook retailers, or directly from the publisher at **www.mmpubs.com**.

 **The Project Management Audio Library**

In a recent CEO survey, the leaders of today's largest corporations identified project management as the top skillset for tomorrow's leaders. In fact, many organizations place their top performers in project management roles to groom them for senior management positions. Project managers represent some of the busiest people around. They are the ones responsible for planning, executing, and controlling most major new business activities.

Expanding upon the successful *Project Management Essentials Library* series of print and electronic books, Multi-Media Publications has launched a new imprint called the *Project Management Audio Library*. Under this new imprint, MMP is publishing audiobooks and recorded seminars focused on professionals who manage individual projects, portfolios of projects, and strategic programmes. The series covers topics including agile project management, risk management, project closeout, interpersonal skills, and other related project management knowledge areas.

This is not going to be just the "same old stuff" on the critical path method, earned value, and resource levelling; rather, the series will have the latest tips and techniques from those who are at the cutting edge of project management research and real-world application.

www.PM-Audiobooks.com

Printed in the United States
215949BV00001B/35/A

9 781895 186758